The
People's
Bible

ROLAND CAP EHLKE
General Editor

ARMIN J. PANNING
New Testament Editor

LYLE ALBRECHT
Manuscript Editor

2 Corinthians

DAVID J. VALLESKEY

NORTHWESTERN PUBLISHING HOUSE
Milwaukee, Wi

The cover and interior illustrations were originally executed by James Tissot (1836-1902). The maps of Paul's journeys were drawn by Dr. John Lawrenz, Saginaw, Michigan.

Library of Congress Card 91-66835
Northwestern Publishing House
1250 N. 113th St., Milwaukee, WI 53226-3284
© 1992 by Northwestern Publishing House.
Published 1992
Printed in the United States of America
ISBN 0-8100-0419-4

CONTENTS

ILLUSTRATIONS

EDITOR'S PREFACE

The People's Bible is just what the name implies — a Bible for the people. It includes the complete text of the Holy Scriptures in the popular New International Version. The commentary following the Scripture sections contains personal applications as well as historical background and explanations of the text.

The authors of *The People's Bible* are men of scholarship and practical insight, gained from years of experience in the teaching and preaching ministries. They have tried to avoid the technical jargon which limits so many commentary series to professional Bible scholars.

The most important feature of these books is that they are Christ-centered. Speaking of the Old Testament Scriptures, Jesus himself declared, "These are the Scriptures that testify about me" (John 5:39). Each volume of *The People's Bible* directs our attention to Jesus Christ. He is the center of the entire Bible. He is our only Savior.

The commentaries also have maps, illustrations and archeological information when appropriate. All the books include running heads to direct the reader to the passage he is looking for.

This commentary series was initiated by the Commission on Christian Literature of the Wisconsin Evangelical Lutheran Synod.

It is our prayer that this endeavor may continue as it began. We dedicate these volumes to the glory of God and to the good of his people.

Roland Cap Ehlke

"... the same veil remains when the old covenant
is read.... only in Christ is it taken away."

SECOND CORINTHIANS
INTRODUCTION

Those who embark on a study of 2 Corinthians will soon discover they are in for a real spiritual treat. The well-known Lutheran commentator, R. C. Lenski, speaks of Paul baring his heart and his life in 2 Corinthians as he does in none of his other letters. It is not the easiest of Paul's epistles to understand, but a careful and prayerful study will result in a bountiful harvest of growth in grace and spiritual knowledge.

The City

Corinth was one of Paul's major mission posts. He spent one-and-a-half years there on his second missionary journey. From what the book of Acts tells us, only in Ephesus did Paul work for a longer period of time.

It was a strategically situated city, lying on a narrow isthmus that separated the Aegean Sea, which lay between Greece and Asia Minor (modern-day Turkey), from the Adriatic, the sea between Greece and Italy. Much east-west commerce moved across this narrow isthmus. Ships were unloaded on one side and then loaded again onto ships docked on the other side. If the ships were small enough, they were pulled across the isthmus, cargo and all, on a system of rollers.

Because Corinth was a center of commerce, many people from many different cultures and countries passed through it.

Those who had the opportunity to hear the gospel while in Corinth could then take it with them to their homes. This was a key factor in the spread of the message of Christianity. One man, Paul, could not do it all. The gospel would have to be brought to others by those who heard it.

Corinth, partly because it was in such a key location, was a large, prosperous, cosmopolitan city. Already in 1200 B.C. it was called "wealthy Corinth" by the Greek poet Homer. Destroyed by the Romans in 146 B.C., it had been reestablished in 44 B.C. by Julius Caesar and shortly thereafter extensively rebuilt by Caesar Augustus. In 27 B.C. it was made the capital of one of the two provinces of Greece, that of Achaia. At the time of Paul, historians tell us that it was the fourth largest city in the Roman empire, with a population of 200,000-250,000.

The city contained at least twelve heathen temples, the most infamous being the temple dedicated to the worship of Aphrodite, the goddess of love. More than one thousand "sacred" prostitutes plied their trade at this temple as a part of the worship of Aphrodite. Immorality, in fact, permeated the entire fabric of Corinthian society. At the time of Paul "to corinthianize" meant to live like a Corinthian in the practice of sexual immorality. If a Corinthian was depicted in a Greek play, he was usually shown as a drunk or a prostitute.

Paul's Work in Corinth

It was to this prosperous, but idolatrous and immoral, city that Paul came with the gospel at the end of his second missionary journey (cf. Acts 18:1-18). Paul had encountered some difficult times on this journey. Responding to a vision in which a man from Macedonia (the other province of Greece) had begged, "Come over to Macedonia and help us" (Acts 16:9), Paul had brought the gospel to Europe for the first time. In Philippi, though, he was beaten and imprisoned. He was forced to leave both Thessalonica and Berea. And in Athens scoffers ridiculed his preaching about the resurrection.

Corinth was his next stop. There the Lord provided some much-needed encouragement to Paul by assuring him in a vision, "Do not be afraid; keep on speaking, do not be silent. For I am with you, and no one is going to attack and harm you, because I have many people in this city" (Acts 18:9,10).

Paul did stay and teach the Word for one-and-a-half years, and through that gospel preaching the Holy Spirit gathered together a congregation of Jews (even a ruler of the synagogue) and Gentiles. An attempt to silence him failed when the Roman ruler, Gallio, who served as proconsul of Achaia from about 51 to 52 A.D., ruled that Christianity was a sect of Judaism. Since Judaism was a religion permitted by Roman law, the same would apply to Christianity. Hence Corinth was one of the few places that Paul was able to leave voluntarily, rather than by force. God keeps his promises.

The Corinthian Congregation

From Paul's first letter to the Corinthians we learn a number of things about the congregation at Corinth. For one thing, few of its members were from the upper level of Corinthian society. Paul writes, "Not many of you were wise by human standards; not many were influential; not many were of noble birth" (1 Corinthians 1:26). Another factor: Although the congregation consisted largely of people of humble circumstance, its members were highly-gifted. "You do not lack any spiritual gift," Paul tells them (1 Corinthians 1:7; cf. 1 Corinthians 12-14).

Though the gifts of the Spirit were abundantly evident in the congregation, love, the first-fruit of the Spirit, however, was at times conspicuous by its absence. This led Paul to

3

write the well-known "love chapter" of the Bible, 1 Corinthians 13, where he maintains that even if a person should possess every spiritual gift imaginable, if he does not have love he has nothing (1 Corinthians 13:1-3). This lack of love manifested itself in factions or cliques in the congregation (1 Corinthians 1:10-17) and also in Christians going to court against Christians (1 Corinthians 6:1-11).

The lax moral climate of Corinth apparently affected the Corinthian congregation. Paul had to remind them that "the body is not meant for sexual immorality, but for the Lord" (1 Corinthians 6:13). He had to urge them to take swift action in a case of incest which they were allowing to continue without discipline (1 Corinthians 5:1-5).

Post-Second Journey Visits and Letters to Corinth

From a reading of 1 Corinthians it is clear that Paul had a good picture of what was happening in Corinth. Both 1 and 2 Corinthians provide us with some clues about how Paul had been kept informed so that he was able to write in such a specific manner to them. But they are only clues. Nowhere are we given a step-by-step itinerary that takes us from Paul's first visit to Corinth on his second journey to the writing of 1 Corinthians and ultimately also of 2 Corinthians. That is why not all Bible scholars, even conservative ones, agree on the exact sequence of events. What we will sketch below, however, does appear to mesh with the information we are given and is the sequence we will be assuming in the body of this commentary. From time to time in the commentary itself we will present alternatives others have offered and explain why we have opted for the sequence that follows.

1. Paul visits Corinth on his second missionary journey (c. 51,52 A.D.) and establishes a congregation there (Acts 18:1-18).

2. On his third missionary journey (c. 53-57 A.D.) Paul revisits Corinth while he is working in Ephesus across the Aegean Sea from Corinth.

   In 2 Corinthians 12:14 and 13:1,2 Paul writes about a coming third visit to Corinth. This means that, though Acts mentions only one visit prior to the writing of 2 Corinthians, another had to have occurred. The most reasonable surmise is that this happened while Paul was in Ephesus, where he spent almost all of his third missionary journey. Paul is apparently referring to this visit also in 2 Corinthians 2 when he speaks of a "painful visit" he had made to Corinth (2 Corinthians 2:1).

3. Paul, from Ephesus, writes a letter to Corinth, probably in response to what he had seen on his second visit. Paul speaks of this letter in 1 Corinthians: "I have written you in my letter not to associate with sexually immoral people" (1 Corinthians 5:9). Obviously such a letter had to be written before the letter we call 1 Corinthians since he speaks of it in 1 Corinthians. This letter has not been preserved.

4. Paul receives reports of ongoing problems at Corinth, even after his second visit and his letter (cf. 1 Corinthians 1:11; 16:17).

5. Paul, still in Ephesus, writes the letter we today call 1 Corinthians (c. spring 56 A.D.) that speaks directly to those matters troubling the Corinthian congregation. Paul is apparently referring to this letter in 2 Corinthians 2 when he says, "I wrote you out of great distress and anguish of heart and with many tears, not to grieve you but to let you know the depth of my love for you" (2 Corinthians 2:4).

6. Paul leaves Ephesus and, instead of visiting Corinth as he had originally intended, travels north to Troas and from Troas to Macedonia. There he meets Titus who has come

with good news from Corinth. The Corinthians have taken to heart Paul's words in 1 Corinthians, and most — but not all — of the problems have been resolved (2 Corinthians 2:12,13; 7:5-16).

7. Paul writes what we today call 2 Corinthians in response to Titus' report.

8. Paul visits Corinth a third and final time before returning to Jerusalem at the close of his third missionary journey (Acts 20:3; cf. 2 Corinthians 12:14; 13:1,2).

Place and Date of Writing of 2 Corinthians

Paul would have written this letter approximately in the fall of 56 A.D. The place from which he wrote was the province of Macedonia, to the north of Achaia (2 Corinthians 2:13; 7:5; 8:1; 9:2,4).

Author

We have been assuming Pauline authorship in this introduction — for good reason. In the very first verse the author identifies himself as "Paul, an apostle of Christ Jesus" (2 Corinthians 1:1), and in 10:1 he speaks of himself in the first person, "I, Paul." The early church unanimously attributed authorship of this letter to Paul.

Purpose for Writing

A three-fold purpose can be discerned, for the letter is clearly divided by subject matter into three different sections. First, Paul feels a need to defend to the Corinthians his change in itinerary. Why hadn't he come to them right from Ephesus as he had indicated he would? Second, Paul uses this letter to urge them to complete the offering for the church in Jerusalem, for he was about to set sail for Jerusalem with the offering. Third, since there were still some small pockets of opposition to Paul, he feels the need to defend his apostleship against these opponents, these self-styled "super-apostles," both for their souls' sake and for the sake of those whom they might lead astray.

Outline

Greeting and Thanksgiving (1:1-11)
A. Greeting (1:1,2)
B. Comforted to be Comforters (1:3-7)
C. Paul's Comfort in His Asian Afflictions (1:8-11)

Part One: A Look to the Past — Paul Explains His Change of Itinerary and in the Process Extols the Glory of the Ministry (1:12-7:16)

A. Paul's Change of Travel Plans (1:12-2:13)
   1. Paul's Straightforwardness in Dealing with the Corinthians (1:12-14)
   2. Paul Charged with Fickleness (1:15-22)
   3. The Reason for Paul's Change in Plans (1:23-2:4)
   4. Forgiveness for the Offender (2:5-11)
   5. No Rest for Paul at Troas (2:12,13)
B. The Glory of the Ministry of the New Covenant (2:14-7:4)
   1. The Ministry of the New Covenant Surpasses the Ministry of the Old Covenant (2:14-4:6)
      a. The Triumph of the Ministry of the New Covenant (2:14-3:3)
      b. The Superiority of the Ministry of the New Covenant (3:4-18)
      c. The Simple Message of the Ministry of the New Covenant (4:1-6)

GREETING AND THANKSGIVING
(1:1-11)

Greeting

1 **Paul, an apostle of Christ Jesus by the will of God, and Timothy our brother,**
To the church of God in Corinth, together with all the saints throughout Achaia:

The opening verses are typical of letters of Paul. He follows the common literary format of the day. First he identifies the writer of the letter, *Paul* and *Timothy*. Then he mentions the letter's recipients, *the church of God in Corinth*. After that comes a word of greeting.

Paul identifies himself as an *apostle of Christ Jesus*. Later in the letter he will have some strong words to say about some who evidently considered themselves to be more of an apostle than was Paul.

Paul had every reason to call himself an apostle, literally "one sent out" as an authoritative messenger of Christ. He had not walked and talked with Jesus during the three years of Jesus' ministry, but the risen Jesus had appeared to him and spoken to him on the Damascus Road. He had not been a part of the group that had received Jesus' Easter evening commission, "As the Father has sent me, I am sending you. . . . If you forgive anyone his sins, they are forgiven; if you do not forgive them, they are not forgiven" (John 20:21,23). He had been given, however, the same commission by Jesus at the time of his conversion. Jesus had told him: "I am sending you [to the Gentiles] to open their eyes and turn them from darkness to light, and from the power of Satan to God, so that they may receive forgiveness of sins and a place among those who are sanctified by faith in me" (Acts 26:17-18).

Paul, therefore, does not have to hesitate to call himself, as he does in this greeting, an apostle *by the will of God*. He hadn't applied for the job. God's Son, the risen Christ, had called him to it just as he had called Paul to a new life from the unbelief in which he had been living.

Timothy is also mentioned in the greeting, as he is in five other Pauline letters (1 Thessalonians 1:1; 2 Thessalonians 1:1; Colossians 1:1; Philemon 1:1; Philippians 1:1). In each of these cases, as here in 2 Corinthians, Timothy appears to be not so much a co-author as a co-sender of the letter. Timothy, along with Silas, had worked with Paul in Corinth (Acts 18:5) and also had been sent by Paul from Ephesus to Corinth a few years later (1 Corinthians 4:17; 16:10) and was therefore well-known to the believers in Corinth.

Paul calls Timothy *our brother,* a reminder of the close faith-bond that believers in Jesus enjoy. They become a part of the family of God. Through Jesus, God is our Father, and we are brothers and sisters of one another.

The letter is addressed *To the church of God in Corinth.* The word translated as "church" was a familiar one to the Greek-speaking people of Paul's day. It meant an assembly of some sort. In the book of Acts, for example, the city clerk of Ephesus quieted a riotous mob by telling it that any grievances against Paul must be settled in a "legal assembly" (Acts 19:39). In his greeting, Paul makes it clear what kind of assembly he is speaking of: the assembly that God has gathered together, all those in Corinth who through the gospel have been brought to faith in Jesus Christ.

And not just those in Corinth, but *all the saints throughout Achaia*. Saints is another word for Christians, those whom the Holy Spirit has set apart from the unbelieving world and brought into a new fellowship with Jesus. Recognizing that those to whom he is writing are saints will affect the way Paul speaks to them. It has the same effect on us as we relate to one another within the Body of Christ.

Achaia was the province of which Corinth was the capital. During Paul's one-and-a-half years in Corinth the gospel had spread beyond the city limits. We do not know to what degree other congregations had been established in Achaia. We do know, however, of believers in at least two Achaian cities. One of those cities was Athens. Though Paul's work there had been relatively unsuccessful, some had come to faith (Acts 17:33). And a congregation had been established in one of the ports of Corinth, the city of Cenchrea (Romans 16:1).

2Grace and peace to you from God our Father and the Lord Jesus Christ.

The normal Greek word of greeting was similar in sound to the word translated as "grace." That word was the equivalent of our English, "Greetings!" "Grace," of course, is much deeper than that: May God's unmerited love and favor, freely given through Jesus, be with you! With grace comes *peace*. Paul writes to the Romans, "Since we have been justified through faith, we have peace with God through our Lord Jesus Christ" (Romans 5:1). With this prayer for grace and peace Paul is ready to begin his letter to the Corinthians.

Comforted to Be Comforters

³Praise be to the God and Father of our Lord Jesus Christ, the Father of compassion and the God of all comfort, ⁴who comforts us in all our troubles, so that we can comfort those in any trouble with the comfort we ourselves have received from God.

Paul usually begins his letters with thanksgiving, as he does here in 2 Corinthians. Later in the letter, especially in chapters 10-13, he is going to speak in strong terms about some problems that still exist in the congregation, but he begins with praise to God. We can learn here from Paul to cultivate a spirit of praise and thanksgiving in our lives. No problems are so great, no situation is so bad, that one has nothing for which to be thankful to God.

Note that Paul calls God not only the *Father,* but the *God* of our Lord Jesus Christ. Perhaps since it is somewhat difficult to understand the phrase "the God of our Lord Jesus Christ," some translate this way: "Blessed be God, even the Father of our Lord Jesus Christ" (KJV). While this is a possible translation, the way it is put in the NIV follows the original Greek text more closely. It reminds us that God is the God of Jesus also, that is, according to his human nature.

Paul first describes God as *the Father of compassion.* This may remind us of Psalm 103 where David writes, "As a father has compassion on his children, so the LORD has compassion on those who fear him" (Psalm 103:13).

He further describes God as *the God of all comfort.* Comfort is the key word in this section. In the NIV translation it is found nine times within verses 3-7. It comes from a Greek word which has a broad range of meanings. It can mean to urge, to admonish, to exhort, to encourage, to counsel, to comfort. It is the word Jesus uses in the Gospel of John for the Holy Spirit, the "Paraclete," that is, the Comforter or Counselor. This is what God is, the Comforter.

Note the word *all*. God is *the God of all comfort*. All real comfort and encouragement comes from the God "who did not spare his own Son, but gave him up for us all" and who will also "along with him, graciously give us all things" (Romans 8:32). And this comfort is there for every occasion.

Paul is going to speak about a personal experience of God's comfort in verses 8-11, but first he wants his readers to remember that this comfort is available for them also. God comforts us, he says, *in all our troubles*. On his first missionary journey Paul had told the believers in Galatia, "We must go through many hardships to enter the kingdom of God" (Acts 14:22). Here he assures us that in the midst of these troubles or hardships, God's comfort is present. And it is present in *all* our troubles.

Paul doesn't go into detail in these verses about how God comforts us. In verses 8-11 he will speak of one way God does this: He may rescue us from our troubles. Or he may give us the strength to bear up under them. Or he will point us to such promises as the one in Romans 8, that "in all things God works for the good of those who love him" (Romans 8:28).

In the last phrase of verse 4 Paul speaks of another significant way by which God's comfort gets applied to God's children. God comforts his children in all their troubles *so that we can comfort those in any trouble with the comfort we ourselves have received from God*. With these words Paul is moving from the vertical dimension of fellowship to the horizontal dimension. It is important for the Christian to remember that when the Holy Spirit brings a person into the

Church, when he attaches a person to Christ, the Head, he is also attaching that individual to the rest of Christ's Body. God comforts us with the forgiveness of sins and with all his other promises, not only so we can be comforted, but also so we can now be comforters of others.

In the next few verses Paul demonstrates this truth from his own ministry.

⁵For just as the sufferings of Christ flow over into our lives, so also through Christ our comfort overflows.

In speaking of *the sufferings of Christ,* Paul is talking about the Christian's cross, the suffering that a Christian endures for the sake of Christ. In his letter to the Philippians Paul calls it "sharing in his [Christ's] sufferings" (Philippians 3:10). Paul had tasted more than the normal share of such suffering. He had experienced an overflowing amount of it, some of it in connection with his ministry to the Corinthians. But the comfort he had received from Christ in the midst of his suffering was also overflowing. Whatever the suffering, the comfort and strength Christ gave always more than matched it.

That was a great blessing and not just for Paul. He goes on:

⁶If we are distressed, it is for your comfort and salvation; if we are comforted, it is for your comfort, which produces in you patient endurance of the same sufferings we suffer.

Notice the two "ifs," *If we are distressed,* and *if we are comforted.* The original Greek makes it clear that these things were actually occurring in Paul's life. He was experiencing both affliction and distress and God's comfort in that affliction and distress. And in both cases the Corinthians were the beneficiaries.

While Paul was enduring all sorts of distress in his ministry among the Corinthians (he will give some examples later in the letter), they were receiving the comforting good news of forgiveness of sins and salvation. If he had altered his message to escape affliction, or if he had given up altogether, the Corinthians would have been the losers.

When Paul personally experienced God's comfort in the midst of his affliction and was given the strength to endure patiently, this equipped him to be a comforter of the Corinthians when they passed through difficult days so that *patient endurance* might be also effectively at work in them. So, whether Paul was distressed or comforted, the outcome was always the same: It was for the Corinthians' benefit, for their comfort.

7And our hope for you is firm, because we know that just as you share in our sufferings, so also you share in our comfort.

Throughout this whole section Paul has not been saying that God's people will never have to go through suffering and tribulation. Rather, his point has been that the comfort God gives, especially by way of one Christian to another, will carry them through. This had been true in Paul's own life and is a truth the Corinthians could also count on. Our hope for you is *firm,* solid, says Paul. How can he be so confident? We, he says, have been brought through times of suffering and have experienced God's comfort so that when you now face suffering, we can share with you the comfort God has given us.

This serves as a good reminder to Christians today that, as the saying goes, "No man is an island." What God permits to come into our lives — both times of suffering and times of experiencing God's comfort and strengthening — is not meant simply to be a private experience to be savored and treasured by the individual. Whatever God leads us through, whatever he has given us, is meant also to benefit and bless others.

Paul now proceeds to illustrate from an experience in his own life how the Lord does provide his strength and comfort in time of distress.

Paul's Comfort in His Asian Afflictions

8We do not want you to be uninformed, brothers, about the hardships we suffered in the province of Asia. We were under great pressure, far beyond our ability to endure, so that we despaired even of life. 9Indeed, in our hearts we felt the sentence of death.

When Paul says, *We do not want you to be uninformed,* this is another way of saying, "We really want you to know." To know what? To know about the suffering he endured in Asia. Bible scholars differ in their identification of what Paul is referring to in these verses. Asia was a Roman province on the east side of the Aegean Sea. Its capital was Ephesus, where Paul had just recently spent three years. It seems likely that Paul would be thinking back to something that happened while he was in Ephesus, some affliction so severe he didn't think he would come out of it alive.

Since Paul doesn't specifically identify what he is talking about, we have to be somewhat cautious in doing so ourselves, but it would appear that Paul is alluding to the riot in Ephesus shortly before he left the city (Acts 19:23-41). As a result of Paul's gospel ministry in Ephesus, people were turning to the true God and away from idol worship, including that of Artemis, the great goddess of the Ephesians. This put the silversmiths of Ephesus into a bind, since sales of their silver shrines and images had begun to shrink drastically. Under the leadership of the silversmith Demetrius, the craftsmen of Ephesus started a riot. They seized some of Paul's traveling companions and presumably would have seized Paul himself if he had not been protected by some friends. Eventually everything was quieted down by the city clerk, but it certainly had been a life-threatening situation. It is hard to stop a riotous mob from carrying out its will.

That was the situation. Paul then explains why the Lord had permitted it to occur.

⁹But this happened that we might not rely on ourselves but on God, who raises the dead.

There is a saying, "Man's extremity is God's opportunity." One beneficial result of being confronted with "impossible" life situations, as Paul was in Asia, is that they remind us of our need for more power in our lives than we are able to generate on our own. We need the power of one for whom nothing is impossible. That one, of course, is our God. If he can raise the dead, he can do anything.

¹⁰He has delivered us from such a deadly peril, and he will deliver us. On him we have set our hope that he will continue to deliver us, ¹¹as you help us by your prayers.

God did not disappoint Paul in this situation. He *delivered* him *from such a deadly peril*. If we are correct in our assumption that Paul is speaking about the riot in Ephesus, God did this through the common sense argument of the city clerk, who managed to silence the mob, which for two hours had been mindlessly shouting, "Great is Artemis of the Ephesians" (Acts 19:34). He directed them to follow the appropriate legal means to take action against Paul and his companions. And the crowd dispersed.

Paul was convinced that the same God who had rescued him from this life-threatening situation would continue to do so in the future: *He will deliver us. On him we have set our hope that he will continue to deliver us.* Then he adds this significant note: *as you help us by your prayers.* Christians should not underestimate the power of intercessory prayer. A great blessing of intercessory prayer is that distance is no factor. Paul could be in Ephesus or in Rome or in Jerusalem. It didn't matter. The believers living in Corinth could be an effective support system for him no matter how many miles separated them.

When missionaries today are asked, "How can we help you?" their response often is, "Please pray for us. Help us by your prayers." These are not idle words. Intercessory prayer helps.

11Then many will give thanks on our behalf for the gracious favor granted us in answer to the prayers of many.

In these words Paul is pointing to a second kind of intercessory prayer, the prayer of thanksgiving for blessings granted to another. With that he is tying together the thoughts of this whole section that began in verse 3. He started out by praising God for the comfort that he gives to his people in their times of affliction, comfort that often comes through other people of God who have experienced the comfort of God's promises in their own lives.

He has pointed to a specific way by which God's children can bring the comfort of God to fellow believers who are go-

19

ing through difficult times. They can help the afflicted by their prayers. Then, when God helps and comforts the afflicted in response to the prayers of their brothers and sisters, these fellow Christians join their brother or sister in praising the God who comforts us in all our troubles. Note the closeness of true Christian fellowship. I pray that God may comfort a believer who is undergoing affliction. God hears and he is delivered. Then I pray again on the believer's behalf, this time the second kind of intercessory prayer, a prayer of thanksgiving.

PART ONE: A LOOK TO THE PAST — PAUL EXPLAINS HIS CHANGE OF ITINERARY AND IN THE PROCESS EXTOLS THE GLORY OF THE MINISTRY (1:12-7:16)

PAUL'S CHANGE OF TRAVEL PLANS (1:12-2:13)

Paul's Straightforwardness in Dealing with the Corinthians

[12]Now this is our boast: Our conscience testifies that we have conducted ourselves in the world, and especially in our relations with you, in the holiness and sincerity that are from God. We have done so not according to worldly wisdom but according to God's grace.

With these words Paul leads us into the main body of his letter. We sense, as we read them, that some tensions exist or at least have existed between Paul and the congregation at Corinth, for he feels compelled to defend himself. The source of this tension will become more clear as we go on.

This is our boast says Paul. We tend to look upon boasting only in a negative sense. It is certainly true that in many cases boasting is displeasing to God. In 1 Corinthians Paul wrote, "Your boasting is not good" (1 Corinthians 5:6). There is, however, such a thing as godly boasting. Later in 2 Corinthians Paul says, " 'Let him who boasts boast in the Lord.' For it is not the one who commends himself who is approved, but the one whom the Lord commends" (2 Corinthians 10:17,18).

That is what Paul is doing here. His boast is that his conscience is clear in the way he has dealt with the Corinthians. He has conducted himself with godly *holiness* and *sincerity.* His motives have been pure. He has not acted in a self-centered way. One who is being guided and motivated by *worldly wisdom,* that is, by fleshly inclinations and desires, could rightly be accused of being deceitful and self-serving, but not one who is being motivated and empowered by *God's grace.* In 1 Corinthians Paul had said about himself, "By the grace of God I am what I am" (1 Corinthians 15:10). Here his emphasis is: by the grace of God I act the way I act.

At this point Paul has not come right out and stated what the problem is, but he is intimating that in some way he has been accused of being insincere and untrustworthy. He wants the Corinthians to know that such is not the case. The next few verses get a little closer to the problem. Paul is being accused of double-talk in his letters, of saying one thing but meaning something else.

¹³For we do not write you anything you cannot read or understand.

What Paul is writing to them is not something other than what they are reading when they come together for worship. They do not have to read between the lines to determine what Paul really meant. What they are reading they can also *understand.*

The purpose of the writings that come from the pens of Christ's apostles is not to obscure the truth but to reveal it.

One basic principle of biblical interpretation is to take the words in their simple literal sense unless the context and the words themselves make it very clear that they are to be interpreted in a different manner. When Christ calls himself a "gate," for example, in John 10, it is clear that this is to be taken metaphorically. He is not literally a gate. But the principle still stands: Take it literally unless it is amply clear that it must be taken in some symbolical way.

The fact that Paul did not write to the Corinthians anything that they could not understand does not mean that everything he wrote was easy to grasp. Peter, in fact, specifically says about Paul's epistles, "His letters contain some things that are hard to understand" (2 Peter 3:16). But that is something different from saying that they cannot be understood. Some sections just might take a bit more prayerful, careful study than others. Paul alludes to this when he says:

And I hope that, ¹⁴as you have understood us in part, you will come to understand fully that you can boast of us just as we will boast of you in the day of the Lord Jesus.

In 1 Corinthians Paul had said, "Now I know in part" (1 Corinthians 13:12). This is true of every Christian. There will always be room for growth in understanding of the word. That is why Peter urges his readers, "Like newborn babies, crave pure spiritual milk, so that by it you may grow up in your salvation" (1 Peter 2:2).

It is Paul's hope that by a careful reading of his letters the Corinthians' understanding will grow in one particular way. His hope is that *you* [the Corinthians] *can boast of us just as we will boast of you in the day of the Lord Jesus.*

Again we have a hint that all is not, or at least has not been, right between the Corinthians and Paul. Somehow the warm shepherd/flock relationship has been strained. Ideally, on the Last Day, *the day of the Lord Jesus,* Paul will be the Corinthians' cause for boasting, and the Corinthians will be Paul's cause for boasting.

When the Corinthians stand before the one who will come to judge the living and the dead and there confess faith in Jesus Christ, they will be able to do this because of Paul's ministry among them. Paul will be their cause for boasting before the Lord.

And when Paul stands before the same Jesus, he will be able to point to the Corinthians as proof that he was faithful to his ministry. They will be his cause for boasting in the presence of the returning Lord. Paul had written in a similar manner to the Thessalonians: "What is our hope, our joy, or the crown in which we will glory in the presence of our Lord when he comes? Is it not you? Indeed, you are our glory and joy" (1 Thessalonians 2:19,20).

Something was disturbing the fellowship between Paul and the Corinthians and thus threatening to rob both of them of experiencing such joy on that day. Paul's motives were not sincere. His letters couldn't be trusted. That is the impression some were giving. But Paul is confident that these misconceptions can be cleared up, if they have not been already, so that the Corinthians can boast of him and he of them in the day of the Lord Jesus.

Paul Charged with Fickleness

15Because I was confident of this, I planned to visit you first so that you might benefit twice. 16I planned to visit you on my way to Macedonia and to come back to you from Macedonia, and then to have you send me on my way to Judea.

Paul says that he was *confident.* Of what? That the relationship between him and the Corinthians was such that on the day of the Lord Jesus they would be able to boast about each other. Because of this close relationship, this warm, Spirit-worked Christian fellowship, Paul strongly desired to visit the Corinthians before he returned to Jerusalem.

Actually, his original plan had been to visit them twice. Evidently he had told them of this plan during his second visit to them, sometime during his three-year stay in Ephesus, or perhaps he had made this promise in his first letter to them, the one that hasn't been preserved. When his work at Ephesus had come to an end, he would cross the Aegean Sea to Corinth, visit there for a time, and then travel north to Macedonia, probably to revisit the congregations in Berea, Thessalonica, and Philippi. Then he would retrace his steps to Corinth, and from there he would set sail for Jerusalem. In that way the Corinthians would *benefit twice*. They would be doubly favored by not just one, but two visits of Paul.

But as it turned out, Paul changed his travel plans. In 1 Corinthians he informed the Corinthians of this change: "After I go through Macedonia, I will come to you. . . . I do not want to see you now and make only a passing visit; I hope to spend some time with you, if the Lord permits" (1 Corinthians 16:5-7). That, in fact, is just what Paul did. In the book of Acts we are told that, leaving Ephesus, Paul "set out for Macedonia. He traveled through that area, speaking many words of encouragement to the people, and finally arrived in Greece, where he stayed three months" (Acts 20:1-3). He visited Corinth only once, instead of twice as he had originally planned.

This minor change of plans led Paul's enemies to label him fickle and undependable. Paul responds to this charge.

17When I planned this, did I do it lightly? Or do I make my plans in a worldly manner so that in the same breath I say, "Yes, yes" and "No, no"?

When Paul *planned* this, that is, when he told the Corinthians that he intended to visit them twice, on both sides of his visit to Macedonia, did he make this promise lightly? Did he act frivolously? Paul asks, *Do I make my plans in a worldly manner,* literally, "according to the flesh"? To do something according to the flesh means to let self-interest determine one's course of action. One who is being led by the flesh would think nothing of changing his plans if it was to his own selfish benefit to do so. One who is being led by the flesh would have no trouble saying *"Yes, yes"* and *"No, no"* at one and the same time, so that those to whom he makes promises could never tell what he is really saying.

You can never trust someone who is being led by the flesh. That is what Paul's opponents were saying about him. We see here why Paul felt constrained to begin the body of his letter by asserting that he had conducted himself in "holiness" and "sincerity" and that he had not followed the inclinations of fleshly, "worldly wisdom" in his dealings with the Corinthians. Evidently, because Paul's adversaries had been unable to find any big things with which to discredit him, they had latched on to this little thing, this change of travel plans, as an illustration of his fickleness and untrustworthiness.

If you cannot trust him for the little things, their argument apparently ran, then how can you trust him for the big things? That is what makes this seemingly minor issue quite important. If the man is successfully discredited, perhaps his message will be also. That Paul cannot tolerate, for if the Corinthians begin to doubt the trustworthiness of Paul's message, they will begin to doubt the one on whom his message centered, Jesus Christ. He therefore responds in no uncertain terms to these false charges.

¹⁸But as surely as God is faithful, our message to you is not "Yes" and "No."

We see how important this issue is to Paul. He takes an oath on the faithfulness of God that what he says can be trusted. How can the Corinthians be sure of this? As proof that he was worthy of their trust, Paul could have pointed to himself and the virtues of honesty and trustworthiness the Corinthians had observed in him throughout their association with him. But Paul does something better than that. He points the Corinthians to the message of salvation he has brought to them and especially to the heart of that message, God's Son, Jesus Christ, and he reminds them of the effect this message has had on them.

¹⁹For the Son of God, Jesus Christ, who was preached among you by me and Silas and Timothy, was not "Yes" and "No," but in him it has always been "Yes." ²⁰For no matter how many promises God has made, they are "Yes" in Christ. And so through him the "Amen" is spoken by us to the glory of God.

Paul is not so much concerned about himself, about his own reputation, as he is concerned about the reputation of Jesus. That would explain why he does not immediately defend himself and his change of travel plans (he will do this beginning with verse 23). Before that, however, he wants to make sure that the Corinthians in no way doubt the trustworthiness and faithfulness of the Jesus he had brought to them.

When Paul came to Corinth on his second missionary journey, we are told that he "devoted himself exclusively to preaching, testifying to the Jews that Jesus was the Christ" (Acts 18:5). Then, when opposition forced him to leave the synagogue, he went to the Gentiles and "stayed for a year

27

and a half, teaching them the Word of God" (Acts 18:11). In his previous letter Paul had summarized his work among the Corinthians in this way: "I resolved to know nothing while I was with you except Jesus Christ and him crucified" (1 Corinthians 2:2). Paul had been assisted in this work by Silas and Timothy who had joined him in Corinth some time after he had begun his work there (Acts 18:5).

The Corinthians should think back to that time five or six years ago when these men had worked among them. The Jesus they had preached had not been a fickle Jesus. Their message had been that Jesus is the Son of God. There is nothing uncertain about him. Jesus is not both *"Yes" and "No."* He does not talk out of both sides of his mouth so that one cannot be sure what he is really saying. Jesus, the eternal, changeless Son of God, is *"Yes."* The form of the Greek verb used here indicates that this was true in the past and still is true. Jesus, the Son of God, has been and still is "Yes." You can trust him.

No matter how many promises God has made, they are "Yes" in him, that is, in Jesus. Here we have come to the real heart of the matter. The Christian faith is just that. It is faith, trust in the promises of God. It is trust that God is telling the truth when he says, "Whoever believes and is baptized will be saved" (Mark 16:16). It is confidence that when the repentant sinner hears the words of absolution, "Take heart, son; your sins are forgiven" (Matthew 9:2), they really are forgiven because Jesus carried those sins to Calvary and there paid the penalty for them in our place. It is certainty that, even though outward circumstances would seem to deny it, "in all things God works for the good of those who love him" (Romans 8:28). *No matter how many promises God has made, they are "Yes" in Christ.* Believe them. Trust them. Count on them because they are the promises of God, who *in Christ* has been and still is the fulfiller of every promise.

That is one primary point Paul wants to make: You can trust Christ; you can trust God's promises. With the last part of verse 20 Paul adds a further, but closely connected, thought when he says *through him* [Jesus] *the "Amen" is spoken by us to the glory of God.* What happened when Paul and Silas and Timothy preached the message of a Jesus who never changes, of a God who in Christ keeps his promises? The Holy Spirit led both the Corinthians and Paul and his companions to say "Amen" to that message. "Amen" simply means, "It is true."

There is great power in the gospel. Not only is it true in and of itself. Not only does it testify of a never-changing Jesus who can be trusted and of promises of God that never fail. It also has the power within it to move its hearers to trust it, to attach their "Amen" to it.

Paul speaks in a little more detail in the verses that follow about the powerful effects of the gospel.

21Now it is God who makes both us and you stand firm in Christ. He anointed us, 22set his seal of ownership on us, and put his Spirit in our hearts as a deposit, guaranteeing what is to come.

Note that Paul points the Corinthians to God rather than to himself or Silas or Timothy. He is not in any way minimizing the importance of the work he and his fellow workers had done in Corinth. Without their efforts the Corinthians would not have come to know the true God. On the other hand, Paul and Silas and Timothy were just instruments that God used to carry out his work.

Paul speaks of a four-fold work of God. With the words *us* and *our* he includes himself and his fellow missionaries,

Silas and Timothy. First, God *makes both us and you stand firm in Christ.* In the original Greek this is in the present tense and has the idea of ongoing action. God keeps on establishing us, keeps on making us stand firm in Christ. This was important for the present situation. Paul's credibility had been undermined. He wanted the Corinthians to remember that it is really all in God's hands, not his. The same God who had enabled them to say "Amen" to Paul's message would keep on strengthening them in their faith.

With the next three words Paul uses a form of the Greek verb that, rather than emphasizing ongoing action, describes something that has happened. The God who makes us stand firm is the same God who *anointed us* says Paul. Back in Old Testament times God's prophets and priests and kings were often anointed as they began their office, symbolizing a separation unto God. So it was with Paul and the Corinthians and with all believers.

God *set his seal of ownership on us.* A seal identifies and a seal protects. Think of the seal of Pontius Pilate that was to protect the tomb of Jesus from those who might steal his body. In the book of Revelation believers are identified as those with the seal of God on their foreheads (Revelation 9:4).

And, says Paul, *God put his Spirit in our hearts as a deposit, guaranteeing what is to come.* Again, this points the Corinthians to something God had already done for them. It assures them that what God has begun he will complete. *What is to come* is nothing other than the full glories of heaven.

All three of these expressions — anointing, sealing, giving the Spirit as a down payment or deposit — may well refer to the same event, the time when the Corinthians and Paul and his companions were brought into God's kingdom through baptism. Through the gospel the faithful God had awakened faith in their hearts, a faith that says "Amen," "It is true," to

God's message. In baptism God had anointed them, sealed them, and given them the Holy Spirit as a pledge and promise of eternal life. And through the same gospel God would continue to make them stand firm.

Paul's point is clear. Though his message is indispensable, for it is through this message that God carries out his work, Paul himself is not indispensable. God is the doer. And God doesn't change. Nor do his promises in Christ. Whatever the Corinthians might end up thinking about Paul, they shouldn't let that affect their thinking about Jesus. Paul, in effect, is telling the Corinthians, "Don't believe because I have told you and you can trust me; believe because God has told you and you can trust him." Faith and salvation do not depend on the credibility of the messenger but on the credibility of the message.

Having made that clear, Paul is now ready to explain to the Corinthians that they really have no reason to doubt his trustworthiness. He wasn't fickle at all. He had a good reason for changing his travel plans.

The Reason for Paul's Change in Plans

23I call God as my witness that it was in order to spare you that I did not return to Corinth. 24Not that we lord it over your faith, but we work with you for your joy, because it is by faith you stand firm.

As he has done above in verse 18, Paul begins with a solemn oath. It is not that the subject itself, a change in travel plans, is so important, but that his enemies have made so much of it. They are trying to undermine the Corinthians' confidence in the gospel by undermining their confidence in Paul.

Paul makes it clear that it was not the sinful flesh at all but rather a loving concern for the Corinthians that prompt-

31

ed him to alter his travel plans. He wanted to *spare* them. Spare them what? Spare them Paul's presence at a time when there were many problems in the congregation. In 1 Corinthians Paul tells them that he had determined to send Timothy to them (cf. 1 Corinthians 4:17). He could help them straighten out their problems. As for the coming of Paul himself, he wrote, "What do you prefer? Shall I come to you with a whip, or in love and with a gentle spirit?" (1 Corinthians 4:21).

Paul did not want to have to come "with a whip." That would have been a very uncomfortable and unhappy final visit before he left for Jerusalem. Paul adds, lest the Corinthians misunderstand, *not that we lord it over your faith.* If the problems had not been resolved, however, he would have been forced to use the "whip" of the law. This certainly would have been done in love, with the Corinthians' joy in mind. He recognized the Corinthians as fellow believers. He says, *By faith you stand firm.* Yet believers, too, need the law to come to a recognition of their sins that they might experience the joy of forgiveness.

But Paul did not want to have to come at this particular time primarily as a law-preacher. That would have been too much like his previous visit, a visit that he alludes to in the following verses.

2 So I made up my mind that I would not make another painful visit to you. ²For if I grieve you, who is left to make me glad but you whom I have grieved? ³I wrote as I did so that when I came I should not be distressed by those who ought to make me rejoice. I had confidence in all of you, that you would all share my joy. ⁴For I wrote you out of great distress and anguish of heart and with many tears, not to grieve you but to let you know the depth of my love for you.

In these verses Paul mentions both a visit and a letter to the congregation at Corinth.

It is clear that Paul is not referring here to the original visit of one-and-a-half years on his second missionary journey as described in Acts 18. Later in 2 Corinthians Paul speaks about a coming third visit to Corinth (2 Corinthians 12:14; 13:1,2). The visit Paul refers to here, then, would be a second visit, a visit about which we are told nothing in Acts. In the introduction we suggested that Paul made this painful, or sorrowful, visit from Ephesus during his third missionary journey sometime before the writing of 1 Corinthians.

It was a *painful visit* undoubtedly because of the situation Paul discovered in Corinth. A reading of 1 Corinthians describes some of the many problems in that congregation. Paul, it appears, had to come down quite strongly with the law and thus to *grieve* the Corinthians. He did not want to have to do that again.

Following that visit, Paul wrote two letters to Corinth, the first of which we know nothing except for a brief reference in 1 Corinthians, where Paul says, "I have written you in my letter not to associate with sexually immoral people" (1 Corinthians 5:9).

It appears that the letter Paul is referring to in verses 3 and 4 above is the second letter Paul wrote to the congregation in Corinth, the letter we today call 1 Corinthians. He wrote this letter out of great distress and anguish of heart and with many tears.

A number of Bible scholars are of the opinion that 1 Corinthians can hardly be described as that kind of letter. They, therefore, envision another scenario, which, briefly stated, follows this sequence: After the writing of the letter referred to in 1 Corinthians 5:9 and then the writing of 1 Corinthians, Paul visited Corinth and there encountered

33

great opposition, especially on the part of one individual, an individual who is further described in verses 5-11 of this chapter. This is the "painful visit" of verses 1 and 2. Returning to Ephesus, Paul responded with a strongly worded letter, aimed especially at that one individual. This is the letter referred to in verses 3 and 4, the letter written *out of great distress and anguish of heart and with many tears*. Then he wrote 2 Corinthians.

The problem with this approach is that it does not fit in as well with the information we are given in Acts and Corinthians, and it necessitates the introduction of a hypothetical opponent of Paul.

To a large degree, our understanding of the circumstances described in these verses revolves around the identification of the letter written *out of great distress and anguish of heart and with many tears*. It is not at all unreasonable to assume that Paul is referring here to 1 Corinthians. In almost every chapter he deals with serious problems in the church. It is not difficult to picture Paul, the concerned pastor, grieving as he is compelled to write strong words of admonition to this congregation that was gifted in so many ways and yet was so far removed from what God wanted it to be.

To summarize, the interpretation we are following in this commentary is an interpretation which sees the "painful visit" as a visit made before the writing of 1 Corinthians and the letter written out of great distress and anguish as 1 Corinthians.

Before moving on to the next verses, we should note briefly Paul's words at the end of verse 4. He wrote strongly-worded 1 Corinthians, a letter that contained much law, he says, *not to grieve you but to let you know the depth of my love for you*. Love and the law are not incompatible. Churches and preachers which proclaim a theology of love that has no use for the law aren't really showing love. True love means that if your brother sins, you will go and tell him his fault (Matthew 18:15). True love means using the law even if it hurts. But our ultimate goal will not be simply to grieve people, but to point them to the One who has lifted away their grief by giving his life for their sins.

Forgiveness for the Offender

⁵If anyone has caused grief, he has not so much grieved me as he has grieved all of you, to some extent — not to put it too severely. ⁶The punishment inflicted on him by the majority is sufficient for him. ⁷Now instead, you ought to forgive and comfort him, so that he will not be overwhelmed by excessive sorrow. ⁸I urge you, therefore, to reaffirm your love for him.

Paul talks about someone who has *caused grief* both to him and the whole congregation. Some interpreters, as mentioned above, maintain that this is a person who vehemently opposed Paul on a supposed visit that Paul made to Corinth between the writing of 1 and 2 Corinthians.

There is another, and more probable, possibility, however: that this is the same individual Paul refers to in 1 Corinthians 5 where he writes:

It is actually reported that there is sexual immorality among you, and of a kind that does not occur even among pagans: A man has his father's wife. And you are proud! Shouldn't you rather have been filled with grief and have put out of your fellowship the man who did this? Even though I am not physically present, I am with you in spirit. And I have already passed judgment on the one who did this, just as if I were present. When you are assembled in the name of the Lord Jesus and I am with you in spirit, and the power of our Lord Jesus is present, hand this man over to Satan, so that the sinful nature may be destroyed and his spirit saved on the day of the Lord (1 Corinthians 5:1-5).

Such a sin would have, or at least should have, caused grief not just to Paul but to the whole congregation. The congregation could not close its eyes and ignore the situation. It needed to take action, just as Paul had already done from across the Aegean Sea.

What Paul now writes in 2 Corinthians informs us that the church at Corinth had listened to his strongly worded advice. It had inflicted *punishment* on the man. It had carried out the final step of church discipline. It had heeded Paul's admonition to *hand this man over to Satan,* that is, to declare him to be a manifestly impenitent sinner, an unbeliever, who was on his way to hell if he did not repent.

This drastic action achieved its desired effect. The man did repent. Now what should the Corinthians do? Paul says, *You ought to forgive and comfort him, so that he will not be overwhelmed by excessive sorrow. . . . Reaffirm your love for him.* These words remind us that church discipline is not meant to be punitive but remedial. Its purpose is not to punish but to correct, not to drive out but to win back.

The danger always exists that if the church is not quick to forgive the repentant sinner and the members do not make every effort to reaffirm their love for the person, he or she will be *overwhelmed,* literally, "swallowed up," by excessive grief and despair of God's forgiveness. As important as it is to hand over to Satan, to excommunicate, the manifestly impenitent sinner, it is equally important to forgive and welcome back the sinner who repents.

⁹The reason I wrote you was to see if you would stand the test and be obedient in everything.

This incident is a good example of why Paul had changed his travel plans. He did not want to visit the Corinthians while such a matter remained unsettled. In 1 Corinthians he had set the problem before the congregation. It was up to the church to do something about it, to *be obedient in everything* that God willed, even this difficult matter of dealing with an impenitent sinner in their midst. Then Paul would be able to come to Corinth on a glad, rather than a grievous visit.

Today also a mark of devout children of God is that the desire of their hearts is to *be obedient in everything,* not to practice selective obedience. God's children ask, as Paul did on the day of his conversion, "What shall I do, Lord?" (Acts 22:10), and then they gladly walk the way the Lord leads — in everything.

10If you forgive anyone, I also forgive him. And what I have forgiven — if there was anything to forgive — I have forgiven in the sight of Christ for your sake, 11in order that Satan might not outwit us. For we are not unaware of his schemes.

Notice that Paul doesn't say, "I have forgiven this man; therefore, you must forgive him." It is the other way around. It is in the congregation that proper discipline needs to be practiced, including restoration of the repentant sinner. If the congregation forgives, then Paul does too. The hypothetical statement, *And what I have forgiven — if there was anything to forgive — I have forgiven in the sight of Christ for your sake,* assures the Corinthians that he will not act unilaterally apart from them. He will do it for their sake. What they forgive, he also has forgiven. Thus the two, apostle and congregation, work together in harmony in this vital work of carrying out proper discipline in the church.

This is important because Satan is constantly trying to *out-wit* God's people. In the matter of church discipline he can do this in a number of ways. He might tempt the congregation to conclude, "It's none of our business," and thus to do nothing. He might lead the congregation to deal with the sinner in a legalistic rather than loving way. Or, when the sinner repents, as here in 2 Corinthians, he might lead the congregation to refuse to forgive. Satan has all sorts of *schemes*. It is good not to be *unaware* of them.

Throughout the section beginning with 1:12 Paul has been responding to a charge that he is fickle and untrustworthy, a charge that stemmed from his change in travel plans. He has explained that whether or not such a charge is true, it doesn't affect the trustworthiness of his message, since God is always faithful (1:18-22). But then (beginning with 1:23), he has made it clear that this charge was not true. He had not come directly to Corinth from Ephesus because he wanted to give the Corinthians the opportunity to respond on their own to the admonitions of 1 Corinthians. Then he would come to them.

Now Paul tells the Corinthians what he did do instead of traveling directly to Corinth from Ephesus.

No Rest for Paul at Troas

12Now when I went to Troas to preach the gospel of Christ and found that the Lord had opened a door for me, 13I still had no peace of mind, because I did not find my brother Titus there. So I said good-by to them and went on to Macedonia.

Instead of traveling west by ship to Corinth, Paul traveled north by land to Troas. He had visited Troas five or six years previously on his second missionary journey and from Troas had crossed over to Macedonia (Acts 16:8-10). Several months after the writing of 2 Corinthians, Paul would visit

Troas again on his final trip to Jerusalem. It was on this later visit that Paul restored life to Eutychus, who had tumbled to his death from a third story window after falling asleep during Paul's long sermon in a stuffy room (cf. Acts 20:7-11).

On this particular occasion, however, Paul did little or no preaching or evangelizing in Troas, even though he had traveled from Ephesus to Troas fully intending to preach the gospel and even though the Lord had *opened a door* for him. It is hard to picture Paul passing up an opportunity to evangelize, but that apparently is what Paul did here.

Why? *I still had no peace of mind, because I did not find my brother Titus there,* he writes. This is the first mention of Titus. His name will come up again in this letter (cf. 7:6; 8:6,16,23; 12:18). He is not mentioned at all in the book of Acts; therefore, we have to derive our information about him from the epistles of Paul. Unlike Paul, Titus was a Gentile (Galatians 2:1-3), probably a convert of Paul's (Titus 1:4), who faithfully assisted Paul all the way to the end of Paul's ministry (2 Timothy 4:10).

From 2 Corinthians 7:6ff we see why Paul was so anxious to find Titus in Troas. After the writing of 1 Corinthians, Paul had sent Titus to Corinth instead of traveling there himself. The two of them had apparently agreed to meet in Troas so Titus could share with Paul how the Corinthians had reacted to this rather stern letter. When Titus didn't arrive at the apparently agreed upon time, Paul could not concentrate on the work at hand in Troas. The route Titus would follow from Corinth to Troas would bring him through Macedonia. Paul, therefore, crossed over to Macedonia in the hope he would meet Titus as he traveled north from Corinth.

We are given here a glimpse at the pastoral, shepherd heart of Paul. He had found it necessary to be stern with the Corinthians. It had not been easy for him to do this, but it had to be done. Now he was anxious — so anxious he could not concentrate on anything else — to discover how they had responded to his letter of concern.

Paul did meet up with Titus in Macedonia. He will return to this subject at the end of the first major part of this epistle (7:5ff) and tell us how the Corinthians responded to the message of 1 Corinthians. But first there comes what some have termed a long "digression" in which Paul talks about the glory of the ministry of the New Covenant (2:14-7:4). In reality, it is not a digression at all. Paul's real concern, as he waits anxiously for Titus to make his appearance, is that the ministry of the gospel continue to move forward effectively in Corinth. The lengthy section that follows is an assurance that, come what may, the gospel and the ministry of the gospel is effective and powerful no matter what obstacles are placed in front of it.

THE GLORY OF THE MINISTRY
OF THE NEW COVENANT
(2:14-7:4)

We are still in the first of the three major parts of 2 Corinthians, a section that began in 1:12 and concludes at the end of chapter 7. In this lengthy part of his letter, covering over one half of 2 Corinthians, Paul defends his change of itinerary against the charges of those who are trying to discredit his integrity. As we have seen, he is concerned about how people feel about him only to the degree that it affects the way people look upon the gospel of which he is a minister, or servant.

In the subsection before us (2:14-7:4), which forms the major portion of the first part of 2 Corinthians, Paul turns the reader's attention to the ministry of the new covenant. We will be devoting this chapter and the three that follow to a study of this major subsection, under these chapter headings:

1. The ministry of the New Covenant surpasses the ministry of the Old Covenant (2:14-4:6).

2. The ministry of the New Covenant is a treasure in jars of clay (4:7-5:10).

3. The ministry of the New Covenant is a ministry of universal reconciliation (5:11-6:10).

4. The ministry of the New Covenant calls for separation from unbelievers (6:11-7:4).

THE MINISTRY OF THE NEW COVENANT SURPASSES THE MINISTRY OF THE OLD COVENANT
(2:14-4:6)

The Triumph of the Ministry of the New Covenant

¹⁴But thanks be to God, who always leads us in triumphal procession in Christ and through us spreads everywhere the fragrance of the knowledge of him.

The word *but* ties in this verse with what immediately preceded it. So concerned had Paul been about the situation in Corinth that he had been unable to carry on mission work in Troas, even though the Lord had opened a door there for him. In spite of that, Paul wants the Corinthians to know that God's work will get done when and where and how he wants it to get done. For that Paul is thankful to God.

God *always leads us in triumphal procession in Christ,* Paul says. By *us* he is referring to himself and other ministers of the gospel. The word translated "leads in triumphal procession" is a difficult one to translate. In other Greek literature it was used of a triumphant general, leading his captives in a triumphal procession through the city streets.

The one other time this word is used in the New Testament it fits that picture perfectly. In Colossians 2 Paul says of Christ, "Having disarmed the powers and authorities, he made a public spectacle of them, triumphing over them by the cross" (Colossians 2:15). Paul is picturing the triumphant Christ leading the devil and all of the evil angels in a triumphal procession, Christ the conqueror leading the devil as captive.

Here, however, the ones Christ would be leading in triumphal procession would not be his enemies, but those who proclaim the gospel. Some Bible commentators try to maintain the imagery of this word by describing these individuals as those who have been taken captive by the gospel. The King James Version seeks to solve the problem another way — by translating the word as "causes us to triumph," but nowhere else in Greek literature is the word used that way.

It is probably best to take the word here in a more general way and not to press too closely every detail of the picture involved in it. In some way, says Paul, we, that is, Paul and his companions along with all who proclaim the gospel today, are a part of God's triumphal procession. And that has been made possible only *in Christ* who won the victory over Satan in our place.

Through us, Paul says, *God spreads everywhere the fragrance of the knowledge of him,* that is, of Christ. The imagery of the triumphal procession is still in Paul's mind. As the conqueror traveled through the streets of the city, people would burn incense and strew flowers along the way, the odor of both filling the air. Those who spread the gospel are bringing to people a sweet fragrance, the fragrance of the *knowledge* of Christ. The word Paul uses here for "knowledge" is a word that means more than simply intellectual, head knowledge. It means heart knowledge, knowing by experience. What sensation can be more pleasant than knowing Jesus!

15For we are to God the aroma of Christ among those who are being saved and those who are perishing. 16To the one we are the smell of death; to the other, the fragrance of life. And who is equal to such a task?

By *we* Paul means himself and other servants of the gospel. So closely are they identified with the fragrant gospel that they themselves can be called *the aroma of Christ* — for they are the ones who bring the sweet-smelling gospel to others.

But note that Paul says that he and other servants of the gospel are the aroma of Christ *to God*. As he brings out in the next verse, not every person to whom the gospel is brought will consider it to be a sweet-smelling aroma. And not everyone to whom the gospel is brought will look with favor on those who bring the gospel to them: *To the one* [the one who rejects the message] *we are the smell of death; to the other* [the one who accepts the message], *the fragrance of life*. The gospel has great power, power to make alive but also power to kill those who reject it. To some it is a death-odor that brings death; to others a life-odor that brings life.

But as far as God is concerned, when his ministers go out with the gospel, they and the gospel they bring are *the aroma of Christ* both *among those who are being saved,* that is, those who accept the message, and among *those who are perishing,* those who reject the message. In God's eyes, the gospel and those who proclaim it are always a pleasant aroma.

Paul asks, *Who is equal to such a task?* Who is competent to be the bearer of such a powerful life and death message? That is a question anyone called upon to bring the word to others cannot help but ask. What an awesome responsibility this is! Paul's unexpressed answer to this question is that he and his missionary companions are up to the task. Shortly he will point the Corinthians to the source of their competency. But before doing that, Paul does some comparing.

17Unlike so many, we do not peddle the word of God for profit. On the contrary, in Christ we speak before God with sincerity, like men sent from God.

Not everyone who calls himself a minister of the gospel can rightfully say, "I am equal to the task," for there are some who are in it for what they can get rather than for what they can give. *Some peddle the word of God for profit.* Paul uses an interesting word here which the NIV translates as "peddling for profit." It has the idea in it of huckstering, of shady dealing. In the Septuagint (the Greek translation of the Old Testament), for example, this word describes those who mix wine with water but sell it as undiluted wine (Isaiah 1:22).

So, Paul says, there are many hucksters of the gospel who, in the hope of winning more followers for themselves, dilute it or add foreign elements to it to make it more palatable to human reason or behavioral preferences. There are many gospel-hucksters who use their ministry as a "means to financial gain" (1 Timothy 6:5). Later in this letter Paul will have more to say about those in Corinth who peddled the word for profit. These very individuals, in fact, were the ones who were opposing Paul's ministry and spreading slanderous reports about him in an attempt to discredit him. Paul says, "We are not like them."

On the contrary, Paul asserts, *we speak before God with sincerity, like men sent from God.* Paul describes his ministry in three ways. We will follow the order in which they occur in the Greek text, since that flows more logically than the order followed in our English translation. First, he says that he speaks *with sincerity.* This is just the opposite of being a shady huckster or peddler of the gospel. He has no hidden, no ulterior motives. He has much reason to conduct his ministry with sincerity, as he makes clear in the other two descriptions of his ministry.

He speaks as *one sent from God.* Paul was always acutely aware of the fact that one doesn't call himself into the ministry of the gospel. He doesn't choose this ministry for himself. A minister of the gospel is chosen and called by God, either directly, as was Paul, or indirectly through other believers, as, for example, were Silas and Timothy and Titus. Paul knew that he was an apostle "by the will of God" (2 Corinthians 1:1). That was not true about those who were peddling the word of God for profit.

Paul describes his ministry a third way: he speaks *before God*. At all times he realizes that he is responsible to God for the way he carries out his ministry. One day he will have to stand in the presence of God and give him an account. That will affect the way he performs his ministry day by day.

These words of Paul serve as a good summary of the way a faithful servant of the word will seek to carry out his ministry today. He will do it with all sincerity, as a man sent from God who one day will stand in the very presence of God to give an account of his ministry.

Having described the kind of ministry he and his co-workers have sought to carry out, Paul then asks a few questions.

3 **Are we beginning to commend ourselves again? Or do we need, like some people, letters of recommendation to you or from you?**

Not far from Paul's thoughts throughout this whole letter is a small group of opponents whom he will describe in more detail in chapters 10-13. Evidently they had previously charged Paul with boasting about himself (note the word *again*). Paul has just spoken of himself as a part of the triumphal procession of the gospel and has implied that he is competent to carry out the ministry of the gospel. He has described himself as being unlike many who claim to be ministers of the gospel but are really in it only for self-gain.

Now he anticipates the reaction of his opponents, those false ministers who are peddling the word of God for profit: "There he goes again, boasting about himself." The answer to the question, *Are we beginning to commend ourselves again?* is obviously, "Not at all."

In fact, Paul goes on, it is these false ministers (later he will call them "super-apostles") who have felt the need for commendation. These are the *some people* he refers to in this verse who needed *letters of recommendation* to and from the Corinthians. Evidently when they had come to Corinth, they had brought with them letters of recommendation from some place (Paul doesn't mention who gave them these letters) so that the Corinthian congregation would welcome them. And whenever they left Corinth, they would undoubtedly ask for such a letter from the Corinthians to bring to the next place they visited.

Traveling from place to place with such letters of recommendation in hand was a common practice in Paul's day. Paul himself, in fact, made use of it. At the end of his letter to the Romans, for example, he writes, "I commend to you our sister Phoebe, a servant of the church in Cenchrea" (Romans 16:1). The Christians in Rome did not know Phoebe. Paul's letter of recommendation would help to assure her of a warm welcome when she arrived in Rome.

Paul, then, is not calling the use of letters of recommendation wrong in and of itself. Rather he is saying to the Corinthians, "Those who charge us with blowing our own horn should look to themselves first. What led you Corinthians to welcome such men into your midst? It was because they actually did what they falsely accuse us of doing: They commended themselves to you by means of these letters of recommendation." Paul, though, didn't need such letters of recommendation. Why not?

²You yourselves are our letter, written on our hearts, known and read by everybody. ³You show that you are a letter from Christ, the result of our ministry, written not with ink but with the Spirit of the living God, not on tablets of stone but on tablets of human hearts.

Paul doesn't need official letters of recommendation because he has something much better. The believers in Corinth themselves are Paul's letter. Does Paul have to commend himself? Not at all. He simply can point to the tremendous change that has taken place in the lives of the Corinthians and especially in their status before God. In 1 Corinthians Paul had written:

Do you not know that the wicked will not inherit the kingdom of God? Do not be deceived: Neither the sexually immoral nor idolaters nor adulterers nor male prostitutes nor homosexual offenders nor thieves nor the greedy nor drunkards nor slanderers nor swindlers will inherit the kingdom of God. And that is what some of you were (1 Corinthians 6:9-11).

That was the picture of the Corinthians pre-Paul. In that same section of 1 Corinthians Paul describes the change that had occurred:

But you were washed, you were sanctified, you were justified in the name of the Lord Jesus and by the Spirit of our God (1 Corinthians 6:11).

A people washed clean in baptism, set apart from the unbelieving world, declared righteous and holy in the eyes of God — that was the letter Paul could carry with him everywhere he went. This was a letter *written not with ink . . . on tablets of stone.* This was a letter that had been written by *the*

Spirit of the living God . . . on tablets of human hearts, the hearts of the Corinthians whom the Spirit had re-created into new people in Christ. The Corinthians were "Christ-letters," *the result of our ministry,* says Paul.

Paul carried these letters deep in his heart, for the Corinthians were very dear to him, but he was also ready to display them at a moment's notice, much like proud parents or grandparents are quick to pull out pictures of their children or grandchildren. The Corinthian believers themselves were his credentials. He needed nothing more.

With these words Paul, without specifically saying so, is showing the Corinthians how unwise it would be to accept the message of strangers who had to bring letters of recommendation and in the process to turn away from Paul. Through Paul's gospel preaching the Holy Spirit had made them living letters of recommendation. What they were right now was the result of Paul's ministry. Why, then, should they turn to those bent on destroying that ministry?

The Superiority of the Ministry of the New Covenant

⁴Such confidence as this is ours through Christ before God.

At the end of chapter two Paul had asked, "Who is equal to such a task?" (2:16). Who is competent to be a minister of the gospel? His unspoken reply had been that he and his missionary companions were equal to the task. Now he explains why. He has *confidence,* he says, confidence *before God,* and this confidence is *through Christ.* Christ had both commissioned him and equipped him with the means by which he could carry out his ministry with confidence. He had given to Paul the gospel, which is "the power of God for the salvation of everyone who believes" (Romans 1:16). And he had given him the Holy Spirit who works through the gospel.

Without Christ's commissioning and equipping, Paul, for all of his natural abilities, would have been unqualified for the ministry.

5Not that we are competent in ourselves to claim anything for ourselves, but our competence comes from God.

Many a church sacristy is adorned with a plaque on which is written Martin Luther's Sacristy Prayer:

Lord God, Thou hast made me a pastor and teacher in the Church. Thou seest how unfit I am to administer rightly this great and responsible office; and had I been without Thy aid and counsel I would surely have ruined it all long ago. Therefore do I invoke Thee. How gladly do I desire to yield and consecrate my heart and mouth to this ministry. I desire to teach the congregation. I, too, desire ever to learn and to keep Thy Word my constant companion and to meditate thereupon earnestly. Use me as Thy instrument in Thy service. Only do not Thou forsake me, for if I am left to myself, I will certainly bring it all to destruction.

Our competence comes from God. The second half of this verse should not be forgotten either. It is true, as Luther put it, that "if I am left to myself, I will certainly bring it all to destruction." On the other hand, God's called servants who are armed with the gospel can carry out their ministry with utmost confidence, because o*ur competence comes from God.*

6He has made us competent as ministers of a new covenant — not of the letter but of the Spirit; for the letter kills, but the Spirit gives life.

With these words Paul begins a thought that he will be developing quite extensively throughout the rest of chapter three. He has much to say about the ministry of the new covenant. In particular his intention is to demonstrate that the ministry of the new covenant is superior to the ministry of the old covenant.

To understand what follows, we should first take a brief look at the words "covenant" and "new." By normal definition a covenant is an agreement or contract between two or more persons, all of whom have some say in setting it up. That is not exactly the meaning, however, of the word translated as "covenant" in these verses. It is the Greek word for "last will and testament," where one person dictates the terms.

The Bauer-Arndt-Gingrich *Greek-English Lexicon of the New Testament* defines this word as "the declaration of one person's will, not the result of an agreement between two parties, like a compact or contract. . . . In the 'covenants' of God, it was God alone who set the conditions." The covenants of God are one-sided covenants. The terms are established fully by God. That is a point we will want to keep in mind in what follows.

Paul says that God has made him competent as a minister, or servant, of a *new* covenant. In the Greek language there are two words for new. One of them refers particularly to time, new in the sense of more recent. The other has in it also the idea of new in quality, new in the sense of being superior to that which is not new. It is this word that is used, for example, in 2 Peter where God's children are promised "a new heaven and a new earth" (2 Peter 3:13) when Jesus returns. This new heaven and new earth will be better than what we have right now. That is the word Paul uses here when he speaks of a new covenant.

Paul goes on to define and to show the difference between the old covenant and the new. The old covenant, Paul says, was *of the letter* while the new is *of the Spirit.* In the verses that follow, Paul will make it clear that he is not speaking about what we today call the Old Testament and the New Testament. Rather, by the covenant *of the letter* he means the law of God, and by the covenant *of the Spirit* he means the gospel.

What is the difference between the two? The *letter,* the law, *kills,* while the *Spirit,* the gospel which conveys the Holy Spirit, *gives life.* Thus they are exact opposites. One destroys, the other creates.

In the verses that follow Paul further differentiates the old covenant from the new.

7Now if the ministry that brought death, which was engraved in letters on stone, came with glory, so that the Israelites could not look steadily at the face of Moses because of its glory, fading though it was, 8will not the ministry of the Spirit be even more glorious? 9If the ministry that condemns men is glorious, how much more glorious is the ministry that brings righteousness! 10For what was glorious has no glory now in comparison with the surpassing glory. 11And if what was fading away came with glory, how much greater is the glory of that which lasts!

Paul leaves no doubt in our minds that by the old covenant he means the law, for he describes it as *engraved in letters on stone,* an expression that takes us back to Mt. Sinai. This probably explains Paul's rather unusual way of expressing himself back in verse 3, where he described the Corinthians as living letters *written not with ink . . . on tablets* [literally, "stone tablets"] *of human hearts.* One would think that Paul would have spoken of writing with ink on paper or parchment, not on stone tablets. But evidently Paul was already at that point beginning to shade over into the subject matter now before us, namely, the difference between the old covenant and the new.

Before we look at the marked differences between these two covenants, we should take note of the fact that both of them were *glorious* covenants. This is only to be expected, since God is the author and giver of both covenants. Paul illustrates the glory of the old covenant by reminding his readers of the appearance of Moses after he came down from Mt. Sinai. The book of Exodus tells us that "his face was radiant because he had spoken with the Lord" (Exodus 34:29). Paul reminds the Corinthians that *the Israelites could not look steadily at the face of Moses because of its glory.*

The law, the old covenant, is glorious. It has its place. Paul tells Timothy, "The law is good if one uses it properly" (1 Timothy 1:8). The new covenant, however, is decidedly more glorious and thus the superior of the two. Paul lists three ways in which the new covenant is more glorious than the old and therefore superior to it:

1. The old covenant, the law, is *the ministry that brought death;* the new covenant, the gospel, is *the ministry of the Spirit,* the ministry that brings the Holy Spirit, who is "the Lord and Giver of life" (Nicene Creed).

    Paul tells the Romans, "Through the law we become conscious of sin" (Romans 3:20), and "the wages of sin is death" (Romans 6:23). The law, even with all its glory, could do only one thing: it brought death. Only the gospel, the good news of the Savior, brings the Spirit and life.

53

2. The old covenant, the law, is *the ministry that condemns men;* the new covenant, the gospel, is *the ministry that brings righteousness.*

In Galatians Paul writes, "Cursed [that is, under God's condemnation] is everyone who does not continue to do everything written in the Book of the Law" (Galatians 3:10). Since no one has fully followed the law, "no one will be declared righteous in his [God's] sight by observing the law" (Romans 3:20). The gospel says, "Another has been righteous in your place. His righteousness is your righteousness."

3. The glory of the old covenant, the law, faded away; the glory of the new covenant, the gospel, never fades.

Paul puts it this way (verse 11): *If what was fading away came with glory, how much greater is the glory of that which lasts!*

This last point Paul will amplify somewhat in the verses that follow. But before proceeding to them, we should reiterate: Paul is not saying that the law is bad and the gospel good. Both are from God; both are therefore good. But, as Paul puts it in verse 10, *What was glorious* [the law] *has no glory now in comparison with the surpassing glory* [the gospel].

And that is the ministry Paul is in. He is a minister of the *new* covenant. It doesn't mean that he doesn't use the law, but he will use it primarily in its killing purpose — to point out to people their absolute inability to pull themselves up to God by their own bootstraps. He will do this so people's hearts will be prepared to hear the good news that brings the Spirit, righteousness, and life.

C. F. W. Walther in his classic book, *Law and Gospel,* shows that he grasped well the point Paul is making here. In the final thesis of this book Walther states: "The Word of God is not rightly divided when the person teaching it does not allow the Gospel to have a general predominance in his teaching." That is what it means to be a minister of the gospel, of the new covenant.

Paul now returns to the picture of the fading glory of the face of Moses he had mentioned in verse 7 and draws some spiritual truths from it.

12Therefore, since we have such a hope, we are very bold. 13We are not like Moses, who would put a veil over his face to keep the Israelites from gazing at it while the radiance was fading away.

The *hope* Paul speaks of is the hope that is centered in the message of the new covenant. It is a most powerful, effective message. It bestows the Holy Spirit and imparts righteousness and life; therefore a minister of the new covenant can be very open and bold in his approach to people, unlike the way Moses, the law-giver, had to deal with the Israelites at Sinai. We are told in Exodus that "when Moses finished speaking to them, he put a veil over his face" (Exodus 34:33).

Paul explains why Moses did that: *to keep the Israelites from gazing at it while the radiance was fading.* It was a symbolic way of demonstrating that the ministry of the old covenant, the law, as glorious as it was, was not as splendid as the ministry of the new covenant, the ministry of the gospel. Moses, in his role as minister of the old covenant, could not be as bold as Paul and other ministers of the new covenant. He had to put a veil over his face because the splendor of the law was a fading splendor.

14But their minds were made dull, for to this day the same veil remains when the old covenant is read. It has not been removed, because only in Christ is it taken away. 15Even to this day when Moses is read, a veil covers their hearts. 16But whenever anyone turns to the Lord, the veil is taken away.

In these verses Paul's focus changes somewhat, but he continues with the illustration of the veil. This time, though, the veil is something that covers the hearts of the Jews rather than the face of Moses. In both cases, though, the effect of the veil was the same: It prevented proper vision.

Their minds were made dull, literally, were hardened. Whose minds were hardened? The minds of the Israelites beneath Mt. Sinai. Paul implies that they should have grasped the significance of the veiling of Moses' face. They should have realized that the old covenant, as glorious as it was, was temporary. But that they had refused to accept. Eventually, in judgment, the Lord hardened their hearts in unbelief.

Their descendants have fared no better, says Paul, *for to this day the same veil remains when the old covenant is read.* Paul is picturing a typical synagogue service of his day, which would always include a public reading of some part of the law of Moses. Sad to say, the Jews of his day looked upon the law in the same way as the Israelites at the foot of Mt. Sinai. They viewed it as God's final word. They failed to see its temporary, and therefore inadequate, character. *When Moses is read, a veil covers their hearts,* a veil which obscured proper spiritual vision.

Why is that? It is because they had rejected Christ, and *only in Christ is it* [the veil] *taken away.* In their distorted spiritual vision, with a veil over their hearts, the Jews saw the law as the cure-all and end-all. They did not put their faith in the Christ promised them in their Scriptures and consequently not in the Christ who came as promised and who by his life and death, became "the end of the law for righteousness to everyone who believes" (Romans 10:4, NASB).

Anyone who has participated in outreach work realizes that this veil is not just over the hearts of Jews, but of all who have not yet been enlightened by the gospel. It is the natural inclination of all people to view their hope of getting right with God through this veil which makes them see the law way as the way to a right standing with God.

It takes the powerful working of the Holy Spirit through the gospel to tear away this veil so they can see the real truth as it is found in Jesus only. Paul refers to this in the verses that follow.

[17]Now the Lord is the Spirit, and where the Spirit of the Lord is, there is freedom. [18]And we, who with unveiled faces all reflect the Lord's glory, are being transformed into his likeness with ever-increasing glory, which comes from the Lord, who is the Spirit.

With the words, *the Lord is the Spirit,* Paul is apparently saying, "When I talk about turning to the Lord (verse 16), that is, being converted, I am talking about that which only the Holy Spirit accomplishes." The Spirit, through the message of the new covenant, the gospel, removes the veil which distorts proper spiritual vision.

There are two results: First of all, *freedom,* a freedom that has many aspects. There is freedom from the coercion of the law: "If you are led by the Spirit, you are not under law" (Galatians 5:18). There is freedom from the power of sin: "The body of sin [was] done away with, that we should no longer be slaves to sin — because anyone who has died has been freed from sin" (Romans 6:6,7). And there is freedom from death: "The creation itself will be liberated from its bondage to decay and brought into the glorious freedom of the children of God" (Romans 8:21).

A second result: Believers are gradually being transformed into the likeness of God. Paul explains how this occurs when he notes that God's children *with unveiled faces all reflect the Lord's glory.* The veil of spiritual dullness and misunderstanding has been removed. Believers are in this sense like Moses at Mt. Sinai. The glory of the Lord shines on them directly. But they have more than Moses did at Mt. Sinai, for what shines on them is the glory of the Lord that surpasses his glory on Sinai — the glory of the new covenant, the gospel of forgiveness and freedom and life.

That message produces a metamorphosis in the believer, a daily transformation, which the message of the old covenant, the law, could not even begin to do. Once again Paul adds that this *comes from the Lord, who is the Spirit,* the Holy Spirit of God who does his work through the ministry of the new covenant.

It is the message of God's love for the world in Christ that the Spirit uses to produce new people who love God and one another. That is the ministry the Lord had given to Paul. That is the ministry he has given to his church today, a triumphant ministry that accomplishes God's purposes (2:14-3:3), a ministry far superior to the ministry of the old covenant (3:4-18).

In the next verses Paul reminds the Corinthians of his dedication to proclaiming this simple message.

The Simple Message of the Ministry of the New Covenant

4 **Therefore, since through God's mercy we have this ministry, we do not lose heart. [2]Rather, we have renounced secret and shameful ways; we do not use deception, nor do we distort the word of God. On the contrary, by setting forth the**

truth plainly we commend ourselves to every man's conscience in the sight of God.

The first six verses of chapter four serve as somewhat of a bridge between the previous section (that began with 2:14), in which Paul has emphasized that the new covenant is superior to the old, and the one that follows (4:7-5:10), in which Paul turns his attention to the fragile nature of those who serve as ministers of the new covenant.

The chapter starts with the word *therefore,* a word that tells us a conclusion is being reached on the basis of something that has come before. Paul summarizes what has come before with these words: *Through God's mercy we have this ministry.* God has been merciful to Paul, merciful first in that he had brought him, the chief of sinners, to faith and, secondly, in that he had given to him the powerful, effective ministry of the new covenant (cf. 1 Timothy 1:12-15).

His conclusion is this: *We do not lose heart.* In 3:12 Paul had said, "Since we have such a hope, we are very bold." He is saying somewhat the same thing here. Even if things don't always go right, even if his enemies try to destroy his ministry, Paul does not have to become despondent. The gospel will triumph. God the Holy Spirit stands behind it.

Paul goes on: *We have renounced secret and shameful ways; we do not use deception, nor do we distort the word.* He is returning here to the thought expressed at the beginning of this section: "Unlike so many, we do not peddle the word of God for profit" (2:17). Only one who does not have the gospel or who has no confidence in it will have to resort to manipulative, *secret, and shameful ways,* ways that are not open and above board, to win a following.

He gives two closely related explanations of what he means by secret and shameful ways: First, *We do not use deception.*

59

The word translated "deception" literally means "a readiness to do anything," an "end justifies the means" philosophy. This does not conflict with what Paul had told the Corinthians in a previous letter: "I have become all things to all men so that by all possible means I might save some" (1 Corinthians 9:22). A minister of the gospel will try to put himself into another's shoes. He will seek a point of entry, some common meeting ground, which may open the door to an opportunity to bring to the person the saving gospel of Christ.

Using deception would be to pretend one has a certain agenda in mind and then to spring something entirely different on the person. It is using craftiness or trickery to gain an intended result. That apparently is what Paul's opponents, the so-called "super-apostles," were doing. They portrayed themselves as vitally interested in the Corinthians' welfare. Such was hardly the case, as chapters 10-13 of 2 Corinthians clearly bring out.

A second secret and shameful way of carrying out the ministry is to *distort the word of God.* The word translated "distort" also has in it the idea of being deceitful. It was used in connection with adulterating wine. Here the picture is that of doing anything, even changing the message, if that will make it more palatable to the hearer. The opponents of Paul were apparently doing that also.

Paul, on the other hand, had nothing to hide. In his ministry he had been *setting forth the truth plainly,* openly, *to every man's conscience in the sight of God,* to whom he is ultimately accountable. Paul had nothing to conceal either from people or God. His message was always open and transparent. It was a message that healed the guilty conscience, since it was the message of the new covenant, of the good news of forgiveness of sins.

³And even if our gospel is veiled, it is veiled to those who are perishing. ⁴The god of this age has blinded the minds of unbelievers, so that they cannot see the light of the gospel of the glory of Christ, who is the image of God.

Paul has no false illusions, however. He knows that his message will not be accepted by everyone. The veil hangs heavy over the hearts of the unbeliever. This is the doing of *the god of this age,* an obvious reference to Satan, whom Jesus calls "the prince of this world" (John 12:31). Though Christ came to destroy the works of the devil and has accomplished this work (cf. 1 John 3:8), the devil, within certain limits, is still powerful (cf. 1 Peter 5:8).

The devil holds the veil over the hearts of unbelievers *so that they cannot see the light.* What is the light? It is *the gospel.* Paul defines the gospel in this way: It is the message about *the glory of Christ, who is the image of God.* God's greatest glory is to be seen in Christ, who is God incarnate, *the image of God.* On Mt. Sinai Moses saw the glory of God as the giver of the old covenant; in Christ believers see the even greater glory of God as the author and fulfiller of the new covenant. That, of course, the devil wants no one to see. And in many cases he is successful in keeping the veil firmly in place so that the light, which is gospel of the glory of Christ, does not penetrate.

⁵For we do not preach ourselves, but Jesus Christ as Lord, and ourselves as your servants for Jesus' sake. ⁶For God, who said, "Let light shine out of darkness," made his light shine in our hearts to give us the light of the knowledge of the glory of God in the face of Christ.

With these words Paul is apparently coming back to the thoughts expressed in verses one and two, verses three and four being somewhat parenthetical. In verse two Paul had said, "By setting forth the truth plainly we commend ourselves to every man's conscience in the sight of God." In verses three and four he accounts for the fact that, even though he has set forth the truth plainly, not all believe. The devil works hard to keep people from seeing the light.

Now in verse five Paul explains what he means by "setting forth the truth plainly." It is simply a matter of preaching *Jesus Christ as Lord.* Paul uses this expression elsewhere in his letters. In 1 Corinthians he writes, "No one can say, 'Jesus is Lord,' except by the Holy Spirit" (1 Corinthians 12:3). He tells the Philippians that on the Last Day "every tongue [will] confess that Jesus Christ is Lord to the glory of God the Father" (Philippians 2:11). It is the basic Christian confession of faith. In his explanation to the Second Article of the Apostles Creed, Martin Luther puts it the same way: "I believe that Jesus Christ . . . is my Lord."

Paul says, *We do not preach ourselves.* This is again an apparent reference to the way his opponents operated. Using secret and shameful ways, deception and distortion, they were really in it for themselves. In contrast, Paul says that he and his co-workers were not serving themselves; rather they were servants of the Corinthians *for Jesus' sake,* literally, "because of Jesus." In view of all that Jesus had done for them, they were inwardly compelled to preach Jesus to others.

In the final verse of this section, Paul thinks back to what the Lord had done for him. At the time of creation God had said, *Let light shine out of darkness.* That same God had removed the veil from Paul's heart and brought light to it. He defines that light as knowing, that is, personally experiencing, *the glory of God in the face* [or person] *of Christ.*

This appears to be a reference on Paul's part to the day of his conversion when quite literally a light from heaven penetrated the darkness of his heart. On that day he came face to face with God's greatest glory. He saw Jesus and, seeing Jesus, saw the glory of God's love. A light receiver, as Paul was privileged to be that day, cannot help but also be a light reflector (cf. 3:18).

That is why Paul does not lose heart, even though the gospel remains veiled to some. If Jesus Christ could bring light to his dark heart, he could do it for anyone (cf. 1 Timothy 1:16). And Paul's message was Jesus Christ, for Jesus is the heart and center of the new covenant. That is what makes the ministry of the new covenant a triumphant ministry, a ministry that far surpasses the ministry of the old covenant.

All believers today are given that same ministry, some by virtue of a call into the public ministry, but all by virtue of their call as priests of God (cf. 1 Peter 2:9). We, too, can be bold in our proclamation of the message of the new covenant, the good news that *Jesus Christ is Lord*. The message is just as powerful and effective today as then, for it is the message that, unlike the old covenant, never fades away.

THE MINISTRY OF THE NEW COVENANT
IS A TREASURE IN JARS OF CLAY
(4:7-5:10)

The Fragile Nature of the Jars of Clay

7But we have this treasure in jars of clay to show that this all-surpassing power is from God and not from us.

The little word *but* alerts us to the fact that Paul is about to introduce a contrast. His subject matter has been the splendor of the ministry of the new covenant. The message of the new covenant, the gospel, far surpasses the message of the old covenant, the law, because it is able to accomplish what the law cannot do. The gospel is able to turn the natural darkness of the human heart into light as through it the Holy Spirit leads people to know Jesus.

Paul now contrasts this treasure, this splendid, glorious message with those who serve as its messengers. He calls the messengers *jars of clay*. From here to the end of the chapter he talks about the fragile nature of these jars of clay. Then in the first part of chapter five he goes a step farther: He speaks of the mortality of jars of clay. But, as we will see, this is by no means a negative, pessimistic section; for though ministers of the gospel are fragile, mortal jars of clay, God still gets his work done through them.

We have this treasure. By *we* Paul would be referring to all those entrusted with the ministry of the gospel, but, as the verses that follow indicate, he appears here to be speaking primarily of himself. *This treasure* is undoubtedly the gospel, the simple message, "Jesus Christ is Lord" (cf. verse 5). We have this treasure in *jars of clay,* earthenware vessels, vessels that are of a fragile nature. If one drops a pottery vase it breaks.

There is a reason why the Lord deposited the great treasure of the gospel in such a fragile jar of clay as Paul: *to show that this all-surpassing power is from God and not from us.* Paul is saying here much the same thing that he had said in chapter three: "Not that we are competent in ourselves to claim anything for ourselves, but our competence comes from God" (3:5). Paul will bring up this same point in chapter thirteen: "We are weak in him, yet by God's power we will live with him to serve you" (13:4).

Time and again the Lord permitted Paul to undergo great difficulties to impress this truth both upon him and upon those to whom he was bringing the gospel. In Asia Paul had faced persecution of such a severe nature that he felt the end of his life had come. "This happened," he told the Corinthians, "that we might not rely on ourselves but on God who raises the dead" (2 Corinthians 1:9). Later in 2 Corinthians Paul will talk about his "thorn in the flesh." The Lord's response to Paul's prayer that the thorn be taken away from him was, "My grace is sufficient for you, for my power is made perfect in weakness" (12:9).

It is the same kind of lesson the Lord had taught Gideon in the days of the Judges. Gideon was prepared to go up against the Midianites with 32,000 men. The Lord made him pare that number down, first to 10,000 and finally to just 300. And then Gideon was not permitted to arm those 300 with anything more than trumpets and torches concealed in earthenware jars. When the Midianites were routed, it was clear that the Lord had given Israel the victory (cf. Judges 7).

In the next few verses Paul illustrates this truth that ministers of the new covenant are fragile jars of clay whose power comes not from themselves, but from God.

8We are hard pressed on every side, but not crushed; perplexed, but not in despair; 9persecuted, but not abandoned; struck down, but not destroyed.

Note the four antitheses in these verses, each emphasizing the same truth: that Paul is a weak, fragile jar of clay but that the Lord's power is stronger than Paul's weakness. Paul is *hard pressed on every side.* The word translated "hard pressed" has in it the idea of pressure. The Greek verb, in fact, was used for pressing grapes. There were times of great pressure in Paul's ministry. Think of the almost constant opposition he faced. He was never completely *crushed,* however. God always provided "a way out" (1 Corinthians 10:13).

There were times that Paul was *perplexed,* at a loss; but he was never totally at a loss. He was never at wit's end, to the point of utter *despair.*

We are *persecuted,* says Paul. He could already come up with quite a list of persecutions he had endured (cf. 2 Corinthians 11:23-33), and there would be more facing him in the future — ultimately martyrdom — but he had not been, nor would he be *abandoned.* This is the same word Matthew used to translate Jesus' cry on the cross, "My God, my God, why have you forsaken [abandoned] me?" (Matthew 27:46). Because Jesus was abandoned by God on Calvary, those who belong to him will never be abandoned.

Paul had been *struck down,* but he had not been *destroyed.* Think of what happened in Lystra on his first missionary journey. He was stoned by the mob and dragged outside the city where he was left for dead. But "he got up and went back into the city" (Acts 14:20). His enemies struck him down, but they could not destroy him.

In each of these antitheses the point is the same: Paul is weak; he is nothing but a jar of clay. And yet he displays an *all-surpassing power.* That power, he wants the Corinthians to know, comes not from himself but from God who is with him. The hymn writer George Duffield has expressed this truth in the familiar words: "Stand up! — stand up for Jesus! *Stand in his strength alone;* the arm of flesh will fail you; ye dare not trust your own." (TLH 451)

¹⁰We always carry around in our body the death of Jesus, so that the life of Jesus may also be revealed in our body. ¹¹For we who are alive are always being given over to death for Jesus' sake, so that his life may be revealed in our mortal body. ¹²So then, death is at work in us, but life is at work in you.

These words are a further amplification of Paul's statement in verse 7, that "we have this treasure in jars of clay to show that this all-surpassing power is from God and not from us." The emphasis of verses 8 and 9 has been on the fact that God's power has been present beyond measure in the ministry of this fragile jar of clay. In verses 10-12 Paul repeats that truth in a different way and then shows how this directly benefits the Corinthians.

We always carry around in our body the death of Jesus. While he was on earth, Jesus had told his followers, "No servant is greater than his master. If they persecuted me, they will persecute you also" (John 15:20). Paul's constant suffering for Jesus was an echo of the suffering and death Jesus had undergone for him. In Philippians he talks about "the fellowship of sharing in his [Christ's] sufferings, becoming like him in his death" (Philippians 3:10).

Paul does not despair, however, for Jesus not only died but rose. If Paul shared in Christ's dying, if he was persecuted as Christ was, he will also share in his resurrection. Paul says that he always carries around in his body the death of Jesus *so that the life of Jesus may also be revealed in our body*. And he will share in the power of the resurrection life of Jesus even while he is living. "I have come that they may have life, and have it to the full," Jesus assures his followers (John 10:10). The weaker Paul is, the more fully will the resurrection life of Jesus be revealed day by day in his body.

Paul repeats this thought in the next verse: *We who are alive are always being given over to death for Jesus' sake, so that his life may be revealed in our mortal body*. He speaks about being given over to death, of suffering, of being in danger of death for Jesus' sake, that is, for the sake of the gospel of Jesus. Again we see the contrast: Paul is a weak, fragile jar of clay, *always being given over to death*, but in that fragile jar of clay is a precious commodity, the power of the resurrection life of Jesus, the real source of Paul's strength. Again Paul makes clear the purpose of his suffering for the gospel's sake, of his *being given over to death:* It is in order that when people look at Paul they pay little attention to him (After all, what is a cracked, disintegrating jar of clay?) and focus their gaze rather on Christ's life in Paul.

In the final verse of this paragraph Paul draws a conclusion: *So then, death is at work in us, but life is at work in you*. When Paul is weak, when he is *being given over to death for Jesus' sake* (verse 11), then he is strong with the life that Jesus gives. And that life, in turn, is what he gives to the Corinthians.

Ultimately, then, this weak-strong, death-life paradox is for the benefit of those whom Paul serves as a minister of the new covenant. Paul is willing to endure constant suffering for the sake of seeing repentant sinners come to newness of life in Christ. In that Paul was like his Lord who "endured the cross, scorning its shame" (Hebrews 12:2) because he knew the victory it would win for others. To see *life at work* in the Corinthians made it all worthwhile for Paul.

¹³It is written: "I believed; therefore I have spoken." With that same spirit of faith we also believe and therefore speak.

In this verse Paul quotes Psalm 116:10 from the Greek translation of the Old Testament, the Septuagint, to explain further why he persists in his ministry even though it meant a constant tasting of death. The verse Paul quotes summarizes a larger section of the Psalm in which the psalmist talks about three things: great affliction, deliverance, and gratitude for deliverance.

The psalmist had gone through a time of great affliction: "The cords of death entangled me, the anguish of the grave came upon me; I was overcome by trouble and sorrow" (116:3). But then the Lord had delivered him from this affliction: "When I was in great need, he saved me" (116:6). "You, O LORD, have delivered my soul from death, my eyes from tears, my feet from stumbling" (116:8).

He is grateful for that deliverance: "How can I repay the LORD for all his goodness to me?" (116:12). "I will sacrifice a thankoffering to you," he says, "and call on the name of the LORD" (116:17).

Paul summarizes the response of the psalmist's grateful heart with the words before us: *I believed; therefore I have spoken.* Then he applies these words to himself: *With that same spirit of faith we also believe and therefore speak.* Paul's experience as a minister of the new covenant was similar to that of the psalmist's. Paul was suffering affliction. He was being given over to death (verse 11), but he was also constantly being delivered. The *life of Jesus* (verse 10) was being revealed in his mortal body. Paul believed; he continued to trust the Lord in the midst of his afflictions just as the psalmist had done. God never disappointed him just as he had not disappointed the psalmist.

Paul's response to the Lord who constantly delivered him from his afflictions, who had delivered him once and for all from the greatest affliction, the hell-punishment earned by his sins? It is the same as that of the psalmist, a response of gratitude: *I believed; therefore I have spoken.* He cannot help but publicly speak forth the praises of God, even if one day the persecution of enemies of the gospel is so severe that his life is taken from him. He goes on to explain why that is no cause for fear:

14because we know that the one who raised the Lord Jesus from the dead will also raise us with Jesus and present us with you in his presence. 15All this is for your benefit, so that the grace that is reaching more and more people may cause thanksgiving to overflow to the glory of God.

With these words Paul is beginning to shade over into the thought he will be considering in more detail in the verses that follow, all the way through 5:10, in fact: Not only are ministers of the new covenant weak and fragile jars of clay; they are also mortal. They bruise, they break, and eventually they die. But what difference does it make if they experience the ultimate weakness, death, for the sake of the gospel? Death means resurrection. The same God and Father who raised Jesus will raise those who belong to him. Christ "is the firstfruits of those who have fallen asleep" (1 Corinthians

15:20). More will follow. "Because I live," Jesus says, "you also will live" (John 14:19).

God will present us, Paul says, together *with you* [Corinthians] *in his presence.* With these words he returns to his main concern. It doesn't really matter what happens to him. What matters is the eternal destiny of the Corinthians. *All this* — the afflictions, the persecutions, even, if necessary, death for the sake of the gospel — *is for your benefit,* he says. Again Paul reveals his loving, tender, shepherd heart. He is willing to face anything, even death itself, if it results in life being at work in the Corinthians, a new life that begins in time but continues throughout eternity.

At the end of verse 15 Paul speaks of a second purpose of his ministry. Not only does he carry it out for the sake of the Corinthians, but also that God might be glorified. He talks about *the grace that is reaching more and more people* as he and others proclaim the message of the new covenant. That in turn causes *thanksgiving to overflow to the glory of God.* As the number of those who have personally experienced the grace of God in Christ increases, thanksgiving to God increases, and God thereby is glorified to an ever-growing degree.

Paul with these words is returning to the thought with which he had begun this section: Ministers of the gospel have the treasure of the gospel in jars of clay *to show that this all-surpassing power is from God and not from us* (verse 7). Ultimately, all is for the glory of God. How unlike the hucksters of the gospel (2:17), who were in it for what they could get out of it!

16Therefore we do not lose heart. Though outwardly we are wasting away, yet inwardly we are being renewed day by day.

Paul had begun chapter 4 with the words, "Therefore, since through God's mercy we have this ministry, we do not lose heart." Once again, he says, *Therefore we do not lose heart.* This time the "therefore" serves as a conclusion to what he has written in chapter 4. Though he is a weak, fragile jar of clay, *always being given over to death for Jesus' sake* (verse 11), yet he is strong; for the weaker he is the more visible the powerful life of Jesus is in him. That life he has conveyed to the Corinthians through the gospel. As a growing number come to experience this new life, God is glorified.

Therefore, come what may, Paul does not lose heart. Yes, "the outer self" (a literal translation of *outwardly*), the jar of clay, is *wasting away.* That is the only damage, however, any enemy of the gospel can do. Persecutors can harm the body, but they cannot touch the soul, the inner person. As a minister of the gospel proclaims the gospel to himself also, not just to others, the result will bc that the inner self will keep on being *renewed day by day.*

Still thinking of the tribulation he is constantly undergoing for the sake of the gospel, Paul says:

17For our light and momentary troubles are achieving for us an eternal glory that far outweighs them all. 18So we fix our eyes not on what is seen, but on what is unseen. For what is seen is temporary, but what is unseen is eternal.

The word translated *troubles* in verse 17 is a form of the same word Paul used back in verse 8 where the NIV translated it "hard-pressed." The word has in it the idea of pressure. Normally we associate pressure with heaviness. The expressions, "the weight of responsibility" and "the pressure of responsibility," for example, are almost synonymous. But when Paul talks about the pressures, or troubles, of his ministry, he calls them *light*, even the kind of trouble he experienced in Asia which was so severe he thought he was going to die. And he calls these pressures *momentary*, even though in the previous verses he had twice used the word "always" (verses 10,11) to describe the duration of the persecution he faced.

Paul can call his troubles *light* and *momentary* because he looks forward to something that makes them appear light and momentary by comparison. He looks to the glory that awaits him when Jesus returns. That glory will not be *momentary*, but *eternal*. And it *far outweighs* any troubles of the present, making them feel *light* by comparison. In his letter to the Romans, written just a few months after he wrote 2 Corinthians, Paul says something similar: "I consider that our present sufferings are not worth comparing with the glory that will be revealed in us" (Romans 8:18).

As we, God's children today, carry out our ministries of sharing the gospel wherever God puts us, we may in the process face opposition and abuse, of a verbal nature and perhaps even worse. In the midst of these pressures we can do no better than follow Paul's example as expressed at the close of this section and *fix our eyes not on what is seen*, the light and momentary problems, *but on what is unseen*, the eternal weight of glory. *For what is seen is temporary, but what is unseen is eternal.*

The Mortality of the Jars of Clay

Paul has been talking about the fragile nature of those who serve as ministers of the new covenant. They are only jars of clay. Up to this point he has been focusing his attention on how this truth affects their ministry. The fact that they are jars of clay helps to make it clear that whatever results are achieved are due not to them but to the all-surpassing power of God. The power is not in the messenger but in the message.

In 5:1-10 Paul reflects further on a subject that he introduced at the end of chapter 4: the fact that he, as well as all believers, one day will die, since they are but jars of clay. He has already indicated why ministers of the gospel don't have to lose heart, even if they must face martyrdom. Death is followed by resurrection, a resurrection to an eternal glory that far outweighs every tribulation a servant of God might face in this life. In the verses that follow he expands this thought.

5 Now we know that if the earthly tent we live in is destroyed, we have a building from God, an eternal house in heaven, not built by human hands.

Paul changes the picture, broadening it somewhat, but he is still talking about the same subject. He had been using the illustration of jars of clay to picture the outer man. He switches now to the picture of a tent that has been set up here on earth. Our life here on earth, our earthly existence, is like tenting. It is only of a temporary nature. One day our earthly tent-house will be *destroyed*. This is a rather strong word. Possibly Paul uses it since he is still thinking about ministers of the gospel who face persecution and even death in their work. Christ's enemies are capable of actually destroying the tent, of putting to death the minister of the gospel.

This does not cause Paul to falter, however, because, he says, *we know . . . we have a building from God, an eternal house in heaven, not built by human hands.* We *know* this, says Paul. He does not use here the Greek word that means knowing by personal experience, for he has not yet left this tent-house for the *eternal house in heaven.* Paul knows, he is certain, that *an eternal house in heaven* awaits him because that is what God has said. So true and certain, in fact, is this promise of God that Paul can use a present tense verb, "We *have* a building from God," even though he has not yet left the tent-house of his earthly existence. That is how reliable God's promises are. If God says it, God's children *have* it.

What is this *building from God, an eternal house in heaven, not built by human hands?* Many commentators see this as the resurrection body the believer will be privileged to put on when Jesus returns. Supporting this interpretation is the fact that Paul in the next verses talks about being clothed with our heavenly dwelling.

It appears to be better, however, not to take these words in quite so narrow a sense. Since Paul is talking about a future dwelling, it appears preferable to see these words as applying to all the glories of the life to come. The *building from God, an eternal house in heaven, not built by human hands* is another way of saying "heaven." The temporary nature of this tent-house will be replaced by the eternal glories of heaven.

²Meanwhile we groan, longing to be clothed with our heavenly dwelling, ³because when we are clothed, we will not be found naked. ⁴For while we are in this tent, we groan and are burdened, because we do not wish to be unclothed but to be clothed with our heavenly dwelling, so that what is mortal may be swallowed up by life.

Not only is Paul able to accept the fact that one day his earthly tent-house will be destroyed; he longs for that day. In Romans 8 Paul develops this same thought. He writes: "We know that the whole creation has been groaning as in the pains of childbirth right up to the present time. Not only so, but we ourselves, who have the firstfruits of the Spirit, groan inwardly as we wait eagerly for our adoption as sons, the redemption of our bodies" (Romans 8:22,23).

When the earthly tent-house is destroyed, Paul won't be left *naked*. He will have another roof over his head, a *heavenly dwelling*. It will be just as Jesus had told his disciples, "In my Father's house are many rooms. . . . I am going there to prepare a place for you. And if I go and prepare a place for you, I will come back and take you to be with me that you also may be where I am" (John 14:2,3).

Paul's longing for death was not simply a wish *to be unclothed*, that is, to get out of this life with all its attendant problems. Death for Paul, as well as for every Christian, is not an escape. It is entry into life in its fullest dimension. It is being *clothed with our heavenly dwelling*. It is that which is *mortal*, our earthly tent-house, being *swallowed up by life*. It is victory. It is to "be with Christ, which is better by far" (Philippians 1:23).

⁵Now it is God who has made us for this very purpose and has given us the Spirit as a deposit, guaranteeing what is to come.

The NIV translation of this verse does a good job of retaining the emphasis of the original Greek text. In the word order of the Greek text the name of God is put into an emphatic position. So here: *It is God who has made us for this very purpose*. For what purpose? For that which Paul has stated in the previous verse: To be "clothed with our heavenly dwelling so that death may be swallowed up by life."

Only God could make this possible. This he has done by clothing Paul with Jesus' righteousness, a righteousness earned for Paul by Christ through his perfect life and sacrificial death in his place.

God has also *given us the Spirit as a deposit, guaranteeing what is to come*. The words translated *a deposit, guar-*

anteeing what is to come are drawn from just one Greek word, a word Paul had used once before in this letter (cf. 1:22). The word was used by Greek businessmen as the equivalent of our English "down payment," or "deposit." It was the first installment of a total amount due and thus served as a pledge of more to come. The NIV brings that thought out with its explanatory words, *guaranteeing what is to come.*

Paul's point is this: The presence of the Holy Spirit in our hearts is God's personal guarantee of more to come. The gift of the Holy Spirit is God's pledge that one day *what is mortal,* our earthly life, will be *swallowed up by life,* the eternal life that never ends.

How does one know if he or she has been given the Spirit? To rely on feelings is not an accurate gauge, since feelings fluctuate. One day a person may feel that he has the Spirit; another day that feeling may not be there. It is far wiser to rely on the never-fluctuating promises of God. God's Word says that if you have been baptized, you have received the Holy Spirit (cf. Acts 2:38). God's Word also says that if the confession of your heart is "Jesus is Lord," you have received the Holy Spirit, for you cannot have made such a confession apart from the working of the Spirit (cf. 1 Corinthians 12:3).

The Spirit whom God gives as a guarantee of what is to come encourages God's people to continue to carry out their ministries in the face of opposition. No matter what happens, even if the earthly tent is destroyed, there is something better to come.

6Therefore we are always confident and know that as long as we are at home in the body we are away from the Lord. 7We live by faith, not by sight. 8We are confident, I say, and would prefer to be away from the body and at home with the Lord.

A key word in this paragraph is *always*. Paul is *always confident*. He is confident while he is *at home in the body*, living in his earthly tent-house. He has good reason to be confident, for all that time he will be working with the powerful, effective gospel through which God works the mighty work of bringing people the righteousness they need in order to be able to stand before him on the last day.

At the same time Paul is *confident* as he looks ahead to the time when that earthly tent-house will be destroyed, the time when he will be *away from the body*. In fact, given his choice, he prefers that time; for all the while he is at home in the body, he is *away from the Lord* — in this sense: While he is at home in the body he is still living by *faith*. Faith, the Scriptures say elsewhere, "is being sure of what we hope for and certain of what we do not see" (Hebrews 11:2).

But when he is *away from the body,* when he dies, then he will no longer be walking simply by faith, but *by sight*. He will be at *home with the Lord*. If it is a blessed experience to be able to live now *by faith,* how much more blessed will it be to live forever then *by sight!* The apostle John expresses this thought in his First Epistle: "Dear friends, now we are children of God, and what we will be has not yet been made known. But we know that when he appears, we shall be like him, for we shall see him as he is" (1 John 3:2).

Paul reaches this conclusion:

9So we make it our goal to please him, whether we are at home in the body or away from it. 10For we must all appear before the judgment seat of Christ, that each one may receive what is due him for the things done while in the body, whether good or bad.

We make it our goal to please him. In 1 Corinthians Paul had written, "Whatever you do, do it all for the glory of God"

(10:31). About five years after the writing of 2 Corinthians, Paul wrote something similar. He told the Philippians that his goal was "that now as always Christ will be exalted in my body, whether by life or by death" (Philippians 1:20). The Christian life is not a matter of rules and regulations. It is rather a joyful response to the gospel that frees and gives life, a response that says, "Lord, I'm available. Use me, in life and in death, in such a way that Jesus is praised."

As Paul writes about pleasing the Lord, whether in this life (*at home in the body*) or in death (*away from the body*), his thoughts turn to the final coming of Jesus. At this time, he says, *we must all appear before the judgment seat of Christ.* It is a day of inescapable judgment: We *must* appear. It is a day of universal judgment: *All* must appear. It is a day of personal judgment: *Each one* will be judged. No one will get in by holding on to someone else's coattails.

Paul explains the basis for judgment: Each will *receive what is due him for the things done while in the body, whether good or bad.* It is difficult to determine where the final four words, *whether good or bad,* fit into this sentence. There are two possibilities. They can be taken with the verb *receive,* which would give this meaning: Each will receive what is due him — whether good or bad, that is, either heaven or hell — for the things done while in the body.

The other way is to take them the way the NIV apparently has done, to join them to the phrase *the things done while in the body.* That would give this meaning: We must all appear before the judgment seat of Christ, that each one may receive what is due him for the things done while in the body, whether the things were good or bad.

While the former interpretation appears to be preferable, in either case the meaning comes out the same: All must appear before Christ's judgment seat. Each one will be judged. The verdict will be either good or bad, heaven or hell. What each will receive will be in accordance with, or with a view to (a better translation than *what is due him for*) the things he did while in the body, that is, while still in this life. There will be no second chance after this life.

There still remains the question about what Paul means when he says that people will be judged in accordance with the things they did while in the body. At first reading, it might sound as though Paul were saying we will be saved by our works or condemned by our lack of works. Such thoughts, though, would contradict what Paul says elsewhere. In Galatians, written before 2 Corinthians, Paul had declared, "Clearly no one is justified before God by the law, because, 'The righteous will live by faith'" (Galatians 3:11). In Romans, written just a few months after 2 Corinthians, Paul's message is the same: "We maintain that a man is justified by faith apart from observing the law" (Romans 3:28).

Quite clearly Paul wouldn't be saying something completely different here. Paul rather appears to be thinking of the same scene that Jesus pictured when he talked to his disciples about the judgment in Matthew 25: "The King will say to those on his right, 'Come, you who are blessed by my Father; take your inheritance, the kingdom prepared for you since the creation of the world. For I was hungry and you gave me something to eat, I was thirsty and you gave me something to drink, I was a stranger and you invited me in, I needed clothes and you clothed me, I was sick and you looked after me, I was in prison and you came to visit me'" (Matthew 25:34-36). Obviously Jesus is not saying that these good works saved them. The kingdom is an inheritance, he says. An inheritance is a gift, not something earned. Rather, Jesus will point to one's good works, or lack of them, as the outward evidence of faith or lack of it.

Paul is saying the same thing here. At the judgment seat of Christ one will receive either good or bad, not because of, but in accordance with what he has done in the body. The cause of eternal life is not one's works, but the Christ before whose judgment seat we will stand. He himself once stood before a judgment seat, that of Pilate, and then went on to Calvary so that we never have to fear to stand before his judgment seat. "We *have* a building from God. . . . We will not be found naked" (verses 1 and 3). That is Paul's confidence. That is every believer's confidence.

THE MINISTRY OF THE NEW COVENANT
IS A MINISTRY OF
A UNIVERSAL RECONCILIATION
(5:11-6:10)

One Died for All

¹¹**Since, then, we know what it is to fear the Lord, we try to persuade men. What we are is plain to God, and I hope it is also plain to your conscience.**

It is clear from several previous references that Paul's ministry in Corinth was being undermined by certain individuals (cf. 1:15-24; 2:17-3:1; 4:1,2). He never names these people, but later labels them false, "super" apostles (chapters 10-13). Paul, therefore, for the sake of the gospel has felt compelled to defend his ministry. That is the context for understanding the opening verses of the section before us. He wants the Corinthians to know that he has not dealt with them in an underhanded way.

With the words *since, then* Paul is telling us that what follows is an application of what he has just said. At the end of the previous section Paul had reminded his readers, "We must all appear before the judgment seat of Christ" (5:10). Among the "all" who will have to stand before Christ's judgment seat will be Paul. That is a sobering thought, leading Paul to say, *We know what it is to fear the Lord.*

When he thinks of that day, he is filled with a holy awe and reverence for the Christ who will come again as Judge.

That awe and reverence for Christ, fearing the Lord, as he puts it here, leads him to desire to conduct himself in a way that pleases his Lord.

The Corinthians should know that his ministry among them was carried out in such a godly fear of the Lord. He characterizes this ministry as trying to *persuade men*. Trying to persuade them of what? Some commentators interpret these words quite narrowly. They maintain Paul is speaking of trying to persuade people that he, not the "super-apostles," is a true apostle.

It seems preferable, though, to take these words in a broader sense, namely, that Paul is here speaking of his whole disciple-making ministry among the Corinthians. Luke uses this same word in Acts to describe Paul's work in Corinth: "Every Sabbath he reasoned in the synagogue, trying to *persuade* Jews and Greeks" (Acts 18:4). As the following verse in the Acts account brings out, Paul was especially concerned about persuading the Jews to accept Jesus as the Christ, the promised Messiah.

How does this harmonize with Paul's statement in 1 Corinthians, "My message and my preaching were not with wise and persuasive words" (1 Corinthians 2:4)? Paul was aware that tight logic, eloquence, carefully crafted sentences and the like will not succeed in converting people. Conversion is the work of the Holy Spirit; it is not the result of the persuasive arguments of human beings. The gospel is always foolishness to the unbeliever no matter how attractively, compellingly, and persuasively it is packaged.

On the other hand, it is precisely through that message the Holy Spirit works. The one who presents it, therefore, will handle it with holy awe. He will not present it in a half-hearted, careless, slipshod manner and thus obscure the message. Nor will he be content with a one-time proclamation.

Paul wasn't. In the original Greek the verb "persuade" is in the present tense, which has the idea of ongoing action. Paul kept on persuading people with the gospel, the powerful means by which the Holy Spirit touches peoples' hearts.

With Paul, Christians today want to share the gospel with those who do not yet know Christ. These words serve as an encouragement to be both persuasive and persistent in this endeavor.

What we are is plain to God, says Paul. That, of course, is most important. God knew what his motives were. God knew Paul was carrying out his ministry among the Corinthians in the true fear of God, in a desire to follow his will.

Did it really matter, then, how the Corinthians evaluated him? In 1 Corinthians he had written, "I care very little if I am judged by you or by any human court. . . . It is the Lord who judges me" (1 Corinthians 4:3,4). Ultimately, it is only the Lord's judgment that counts. If one has to make the choice between being approved by the Lord or by people, for the Christian the Lord will win out every time.

It doesn't always have to be such an either/or situation, however. Paul's hope is that deep down in their *conscience,* a conscience touched by Paul's preaching of law and gospel, the Corinthians will recognize that Paul has been open and transparent in his dealings with them, that he has nothing to hide.

[12]We are not trying to commend ourselves to you again, but are giving you an opportunity to take pride in us, so that you can answer those who take pride in what is seen rather than in what is in the heart.

Paul realized that he had to choose his words very carefully in this letter. He knew his enemies in Corinth would try their best to turn his words around and make them say precisely the opposite of his intent. Often, as in this verse, he anticipated objections and responded to them. Paul had just said he had nothing to hide either from God or from the Corinthians. He had carried out his ministry of persuading people by the gospel in the fear of the Lord. In the previous chapter he had described his ministry with such statements as, "We commend ourselves to every man's conscience in the sight of God. . . . We do not preach ourselves, but Jesus Christ as Lord. . . . We always carry around in our body the death of Jesus, so that the life of Jesus may also be revealed in our body. . . . Death is at work in us, but life is at work in you" (4:2,5,10,12).

He foresees the accusation: "There he goes again, bragging about himself instead of going about his work in a quiet, humble manner as a real minister of the gospel should do." To neutralize that possible objection, he tells them why he has reminded them about the manner in which he conducted his ministry: He wants to give them an opportunity *to take pride in* (literally, "boast about") him, so they have some ammunition to use in response to his opponents.

Earlier in the letter Paul had written, "This is our boast: Our conscience testifies that we have conducted ourselves in the world, and especially in our relations with you, in the holiness and sincerity that are from God" (1:12). This was a proper, godly boasting about self. Now Paul says there is also such a thing as a proper, godly boasting about another. When Paul's opponents began to put Paul down, the Corinthian believers should respond by "boasting" about Paul. They should point out what Paul was really like.

They should understand that Paul's adversaries were touching only external things in their complaints about him. They *take pride in* [literally, "boast about"] *what is seen rather than in what is in the heart.* Later Paul will discuss this matter in more detail. He will describe, for example, how the "super-apostles" boasted of their heritage, that they were descendants of Abraham (cf. 11:22,23). They also bragged that they were much better public speakers than Paul (cf. 11:6).

But that, obviously, is not what really counts. What is *in the heart* determines the true worth of a minister of Christ. Paul's hope is that his speech and conduct have made it clear that in his heart was a true fear of the Lord and a genuine desire to serve the Corinthians.

13If we are out of our mind, it is for the sake of God; if we are in our right mind, it is for you.

Some years before this, Jesus' unbelieving relatives had exclaimed, as they observed him working such long hours that he couldn't even find time to eat, "He is out of his mind" (Mark 3:21). It is likely that Paul is referring here to something similar. Paul toiled and labored day and night. For the sake of the gospel he permitted himself to be exposed again and again to ridicule, mockery, beatings, stonings, imprisonment (cf. 2 Corinthians 11:23-29). Such tireless zeal could easily have led Paul's detractors to charge him with being a religious fanatic.

Paul's response? "If you want to conclude from what you see that I'm out of my mind, then so be it. But the truth of the matter is I can do nothing else. I do what I do *for the sake of God,* a God who loved me so much that he sent his Son to die for me."

Paul goes on: *If we are in our right mind, it is for you.* Paul's point: He did nothing in his ministry for self-advantage. If he appeared to be out of his mind, it was for the glory of the Lord. And when Paul was quietly and soberly teaching and instructing the Corinthians, it was to benefit them.

¹⁴For Christ's love compels us, because we are convinced that one died for all, and therefore all died. ¹⁵And he died for all, that those who live should no longer live for themselves but for him who died for them and was raised again.

The word *for* ties these verses directly to the immediately preceding verses. It is *Christ's love* that *compels* Paul to labor so intensely that he is charged with being out of his mind. It is Christ's love that compels him to keep on instructing the Corinthians in a sober and sound manner, even if at times his teaching appears to be falling on deaf ears.

The NIV's translation, *Christ's love,* is a good one. The original Greek says, "The love of Christ." This can mean either the love Christ has for us or the love we have for Christ. The question that needs answering, then, is: What is it above all that compels Paul to carry out his ministry with such intensity and devotion? Is it the love he has for Christ? Or is it the love Christ has for him?

In the context of this verse it is apparent that Paul is talking about what precedes the Christian's response of love for Christ. What comes first is Christ's love for him, as expressed in the words *One died for all.*

The word translated *for* can mean "on behalf of" or "for the benefit of." But it can also mean "in the place of" or "instead of," as, for example, in Galatians 3:13: "Christ redeemed us from the curse of the law [eternal death] by becoming a curse for [in the place of] us."

With these words, *One died for all,* Paul is talking about what Christians today call the vicarious, or substitutionary, atonement. Because Christ died in our place, we don't have to die. In fact, because Christ died in our place, we have already died: *One died for all, and therefore all died.* In a very real sense, when Christ died, we died. With Christ's death, our death penalty has been paid.

We need to note especially one word that occurs three times in these two verses, the word *all.* "One died for *all,* and therefore *all* died. . . . He died for *all.*" *All* means just that. No one is excluded. The love of Christ is so broad and boundless it extends to the whole world. When Christ died, the whole world died. There is no one whose sins have not been atoned for. *One died for all.*

Paul is going to expand this thought in the remaining verses of the chapter, but before doing that he makes an application that further explains his dedicated, tireless service as a minister of Christ. Christ died for all, he explains, *that those who live,* that is, believers, who share in the benefits of Christ's death and resurrection, *should no longer live for themselves but for him who died for them and was raised again.*

Christ's death is our death; his resurrection is our resurrection. Christians, who with Christ have died and risen to a brand new life, thus live a "borrowed life," as Prof. J. P. Meyer so nicely puts it in his commentary on 2 Corinthians. It is a life that is marked, not by self-love, but by love for the Christ who loved them first. That explains why Paul sometimes appeared to be almost fanatical in his ministry. He was compelled, not by law, but by love, Christ's love, to live every minute of his existence for him who in his place died and was raised.

Christians today who weary of service in the kingdom, who sense a decline in the fervency of their love for Christ, would do well to come back again and again to the fountain, to the source of a Christian's love and service. We need to return to Calvary and view again the love Christ demonstrated for us where one died and therefore all died. And then, with Christ, we rise to newness of life, living a "borrowed life," his life, to his glory.

The World Was Reconciled to God through Christ

¹⁶So from now on we regard no one from a worldly point of view. Though we once regarded Christ in this way, we do so no longer. ¹⁷Therefore, if anyone is in Christ, he is a new creation; the old has gone, the new has come!

These verses are somewhat transitional in that they form two conclusions to the previous verses (verses 11-15), and they lead into the climactic final verses of the chapter (verses 18-21).

The first conclusion is that Paul no longer looked at people *from a worldly point of view.* To look at people from a worldly point of view means to look only at the surface of things. When Paul looked at people, he no longer simply saw what was right before his eyes, things like outward appearance, age, sex, educational level, income, abilities, and the like. Nor did he view people as objects to be maneuvered and exploited for personal gain. That's looking at people "according to the flesh," a literal translation of *from a worldly point of view.*

Rather Paul viewed people from the perspective of the finished work of Jesus. Jesus' death was their death; Jesus' resurrection was their resurrection. Seeing people in this light, his concern was not for what he could get out of them, but for what he could give them. The best thing he could give them was the message about the Jesus who had died and risen on their behalf. Paul will amplify that thought in the final verses of the chapter.

Paul confesses that he had *once regarded Christ in this way* also, that is, from a worldly point of view. He had looked only on the surface of things and saw a false Messiah, for the Christ he saw didn't match his expectations. He had been brought up to expect a Messiah who would satisfy the desires of his flesh by rescuing him and his people from their political enemies. From Paul's fleshly perspective, the crucifixion of Jesus appeared to be a bitter defeat, not a glorious triumph.

But now by the Spirit he no longer viewed things from the vantage point of the flesh. He saw Jesus as the one who died the death of all and who by his resurrection is the assurance of life to all.

That was one big change which had occurred in Paul's life. He now saw Jesus as the one who had died and been raised to life for all. And when he looked at people, he saw them as a part of the "all" for whom Christ had died and risen.

Paul draws a second conclusion from the truth that Christ died and was raised in the place of all: *If anyone is in Christ, he is a new creation.* The one who is in Christ is the person who by faith has made the death and resurrection of Christ his or her own. God no longer sees the old, pre-Christ person. That, says Paul, *has gone,* and a new person *has come.* The word translated *has come* has in it the idea of something that started in the past and continues into the present. One who is *in Christ* has become, is, and continues to be a new creation in the eyes of God.

Imagine the joy in Paul's heart as he penned these words! Think of what he had been in the past. He reminds Timothy, "I was once a blasphemer and a persecutor and a violent man" (1 Timothy 1:13). But now, because "one died for all," he can confidently say, *The old has gone.* In its place is a *new creation* whom God no longer looks upon as a guilty sinner.

What Paul writes is no less heartwarming to present-day readers. The Scriptures remind us: "At one time we too were foolish, disobedient, deceived and enslaved by all kinds of passions and pleasures. We lived in malice and envy, being hated and hating one another" (Titus 3:3). But now the Christian can say, "The old has gone. In Christ who died in my place and was raised again I am a new creation."

In the verses that follow, Paul elaborates on this marvelous truth and on its worldwide implications.

18All this is from God, who reconciled us to himself through Christ and gave us the ministry of reconciliation: 19that God was reconciling the world to himself in Christ, not counting men's sins against them. And he has committed to us the message of reconciliation.

All this — the love of a Christ who died and rose for all, the miracle of being transformed into a new creation who can now live for the Christ who died and rose for all, a new perspective on life which views Christ and people from the vantage point of the cross and empty tomb — all this, says Paul, is *from God.* In no way could Paul or any human being have accomplished this work.

Paul describes this work of God with the word "reconciliation." God, says Paul, *reconciled us to himself.* This is the first of five times in verses 18-21 that the word "reconcile" or "reconciliation" is used. It is clearly the key word in these verses.

The basic meaning of the word is "to change." Thayer's *Greek-English Lexicon of the New Testament* notes that the earliest use of this word was for "the business of money-changers, exchanging equivalent values." Then it came to

91

mean a change in relationship on the part of people, from a hostile relationship to one of peace and friendship.

Paul uses this word in that way in 1 Corinthians. Writing on the subject of marriage and divorce, he says, "A wife must not separate from her husband. But if she does, she must remain unmarried or else be reconciled to her husband" (1 Corinthians 7:10,11). These two parties at variance with one another, husband and wife, should be restored to a right relationship with each other. They should be reconciled.

Paul uses the word reconcile in a somewhat similar way in the verses before us. In this case the two parties are God and all of humanity. It is obvious that the problem here was caused by only one of the two parties. Using this same word in Romans 5, Paul writes: "When we were God's enemies, we were reconciled to him" (Romans 5:10). We were enemies. God was and always has been love. If a change in relationship were to occur, God would have to take the initiative. This is exactly what happened: *God reconciled us to himself.* He took it upon himself to change our status from enemies to friends.

How did he do it? *Through* Christ, says Paul. In the Romans passage just quoted, Paul explains how God reconciled himself to us through Christ: "We were reconciled to him through the death of his Son" (Romans 5:10). Prof. J. P. Meyer puts it nicely in his commentary on 2 Corinthians:

> If God finds us outside of Christ, he sees us as people who are not only covered over and over with sin, but who are permeated through and through with this poison. But as soon as Christ intervenes, and God looks at us through Christ, then all our sins are screened and blocked out. His all-searching eye finds none, and he pronounces us righteous (p. 108).

God has done something else besides reconciling us to himself through Christ. He also *gave us the ministry of reconciliation.* In the original Greek text these two actions of God are closely tied together. The same God who reconciled us to himself is the one who gave us the ministry of reconciliation, says Paul. The *ministry of reconciliation* is the way by which God gets the message of reconciliation out into the world. God has made us missionaries, we would, perhaps, say today.

Who is meant by the *us* whom God has reconciled to himself through Christ and to whom he has given this ministry of reconciliation? Certainly Paul would include himself and also someone like Timothy whose name is included in the greeting of 2 Corinthians. Ultimately, though, the *us* would refer to all whom the Holy Spirit has led to faith and who thus enjoy the new status of friends, rather than enemies, of God. When by faith we have been led to accept God's work of reconciliation through Christ, along with the gift of faith God gives us a commission: Get the good news of reconciliation out to others. Speaking to all believers, Peter says their call is to "declare the praises of him who called you out of darkness into his wonderful light" (1 Peter 2:9).

There is a good reason for this commission, as the next verse brings out. God's work of reconciliation through Christ was not restricted to a select few: *God was reconciling the world to himself in Christ.* A better translation of this phrase may be, "God was in Christ, reconciling the world to himself," the emphasis being that it was the God-man, Jesus Christ, who reconciled the world to God. This would parallel Paul's words in Colossians: "God was pleased to have all his fullness dwell in him [Christ], and through him to reconcile to himself all things" (Colossians 1:19,20).

Either way, Paul is pointing the reader to the scope of the reconciliation God has effected through Christ. Paul has already said, "One died for all" (verse 14). Now, using the term "the world," which means the same as "all," he speaks of the result of this death for, or in the place of, all: God has reconciled the whole world to himself. And then he explains how he has done this: *not counting men's sins against them.*

The word translated *counting* is a bookkeeping term. It means to credit to someone's account. Here Paul is affirming that God no longer credits sin to the world's account. God has reconciled the world to himself by simply no longer charging the world's sins against the world.

How the God who says, "Cursed is everyone who does not continue to do everything written in the Book of the Law" (Galatians 3:10), can now say, "I no longer count the world's sins against the world," Paul will explain in the final verse of this chapter. But before we move on, we should consider the implications of the verses before us. Paul here is talking about an objective fact, about something that was accomplished when Christ was here on earth. God, through Christ, has brought about a universal reconciliation. He says to the world, and that includes every person in it, yesterday, today, and tomorrow, "I no longer charge your sins against you. In my eyes you are no longer guilty sinners. Your sins have been forgiven."

That makes all the difference in the world for one's own personal assurance of a right standing with God. It is not my repentance and faith that produce forgiveness. If that were the case, then weakness in faith would mean less forgiveness. I could never be sure that my slate is completely clean. Rather, by repentance and faith I receive the full forgiveness already won for the whole world when God in Christ no longer counted the world's sins against the world.

A right understanding of the objective fact of a God-effected universal reconciliation in Christ is important also for those to whom God *has committed . . . the message of reconciliation,* that is, all believers. Our message is not, "If you believe, God will no longer charge your sins against you." It is, "In Christ, what needs to be done has been done. God no longer charges your sins against you. Believe."

Paul speaks of his work as such a messenger in the verse that follows:

20We are therefore Christ's ambassadors, as though God were making his appeal through us. We implore you on Christ's behalf: Be reconciled to God.

An *ambassador* doesn't speak in his own name, he doesn't act on his own authority, and he doesn't communicate his own opinions. He says what he is told to say. He acts on the authority of the one who sent him and speaks in his name.

Paul and his companions were ambassadors. They acted on the authority of their sender, Christ. They spoke in his place and said what he would have said if he himself had been there. The message was a simple one: *Be reconciled to God.*

At first hearing, these words might appear to be contradicting what Paul has just said, that God has already reconciled us and the whole world to himself. Now he talks about the need for us to be reconciled to God.

This is not conflicting testimony at all, however. Rather Paul is guarding against what today is called "universalism," the teaching that one day everyone is going to go to heaven. This idea could well arise if one looked only at the objective side of reconciliation. One might conclude: If God no longer counts the world's sins against the world, then that means everyone in the world will be saved. That such will not be the case is amply testified to throughout the Scriptures. Mark

95

16:16, for example, records the words of Jesus: "Whoever believes and is baptized will be saved, but whoever does not believe will be condemned."

Paul is saying the same thing here with the appeal, *Be reconciled to God.* It is by faith that the individual receives the benefits of the reconciliation God has already accomplished. If one rejects this finished work, one's sins remain on oneself. On the last day God will see those sins and, seeing them, sentence the person to suffer their consequence, eternal death.

This underscores the need to proclaim the gospel throughout the world. All have been reconciled to God. God no longer charges the world's sins against the world. But only those who hear this message and believe it will personally experience the forgiveness and life it offers.

In the first two verses of the next chapter Paul will return to this subject. He will speak of the urgency of clinging in faith to the message of reconciliation. But before doing that, he summarizes in beautiful fashion how a just and holy God can no longer count the world's sins against it.

21God made him who had no sin to be sin for us, so that in him we might become the righteousness of God.

This is God's "Great Exchange." On the one side is Jesus, the one who *had no sin.* The original Greek says that he "knew" no sin. He had experienced temptation many a time. In fact, he had been "tempted in every way, just as we are" (Hebrews 4:15). But he had never succumbed to temptation. He had never personally experienced what it means to sin nor what it means to be a sinner. "He committed no sin, and no deceit was found in his mouth" (1 Peter 2:22). He was the "lamb without blemish or defect" (1 Peter 1:19).

On the other side was *us*. By *us* Paul includes himself and everyone who has ever lived and will ever live. The "us" side is not a pretty picture. In Romans Paul combines several Old Testament passages to paint the picture of "us":

> There is no one righteous, not even one; there is no one who understands, no one who seeks God. All have turned away, they have together become worthless; there is no one who does good, not even one. Their throats are open graves; their tongues practice deceit. The poison of vipers is on their lips. Their mouths are full of cursing and bitterness. Their feet are swift to shed blood; ruin and misery mark their ways, and the way of peace they do not know. There is no fear of God before their eyes (Romans 3:10-18).

On the "us" side is only sin, lack of righteousness, which merits death. On the Jesus side is what the "us" side desperately needs, righteousness, holiness, which gives life.

Then came the exchange: *God made him who had no sin to be sin for us.* Note the words *God made*. Christ's crucifixion on Calvary with the world's sins upon him was no accident. Isaiah writes, "It was the LORD's will to crush him and cause him to suffer" (Isaiah 53:10). The LORD had the world's good in mind. On Calvary Christ's triumphant "It is finished" communicated clearly that the death penalty which the world's sin merited had been paid in full by another.

That's one half of the exchange. The other half: *so that in him we might become the righteousness of God.* God, who because of Christ no longer charges the sins of the world against the world, credits the righteousness, the holiness, of Christ to the world. Christ's righteousness for mankind's sin — a great exchange indeed!

The hymn writer expresses the results of this great exchange:

> Jesus, Thy blood and righteousness
> My beauty are, my glorious dress;
> Midst flaming worlds, in these arrayed,
> With joy shall I lift up my head.
> Bold shall I stand in that great Day,
> For who aught to my charge shall lay?
> Fully through these.[Christ's blood and
> righteousness] absolved I am
> From sin and fear, from guilt and shame.
> (TLH 371:1,2)

As we move ahead into the opening verses of the next chapter, we see that Paul returns to the thought that, though the sins of the world were put on Christ and have been paid for in full, and though Christ's righteousness has been credited to the whole world, unbelief can cause one to lose out on the benefits of this great exchange.

6 **As God's fellow workers we urge you not to receive God's grace in vain.**

It is possible to *receive God's grace in vain.* Think of Jesus' Parable of the Sower. Some of the seed of the word fell on the hard beaten path, some on rocky soil, some among thorns. Only some fell on good ground and sprang up and bore fruit. On the rest, the seed was sown in vain.

From the personal tone of this verse (Paul says, "We urge you"), it is clear that Paul is concerned that some of the Corinthians might be in danger of having received from Paul God's gracious message of salvation in vain. Paul doesn't reveal the specific problem. It is not unlikely that it had something to do with the efforts of Paul's opponents to discredit Paul and thus to discredit his message. If the Corinthians now rejected Paul's message, which centered in God's grace, God's loving-kindness in reconciling the world to himself through Christ, then they would have received God's grace in vain.

Paul, therefore, urges the Corinthians:

2For he says,

> **"In the time of my favor I heard you,**
> **and in the day of salvation I helped you."**

I tell you, now is the time of God's favor, now is the day of salvation.

The first part of this verse is a quotation of Isaiah 49:8 from the Septuagint translation. It is part of a Messianic prophecy. God the Father is talking to his Son, the Messiah. He promises that he will help his Servant, the Messiah, in the day when the message of salvation is offered to the Gentiles.

Paul applies this prophecy to his time: *I tell you, now is the time of God's favor, now is the day of salvation.* His point is this: The Old Testament prophesied the coming of the day of salvation for the Gentiles, the time when the message of God's grace would be brought to them. That time has come, says Paul. Don't lose out on what it offers by rejecting the gospel. Don't receive God's grace in vain. Receive it and keep on clinging to it in faith.

These verses serve as a strong reminder to us today that our proclamation of the gospel must also sound such a note of urgency. Today, too, is the time of God's favor, the day of salvation. Tomorrow is the judgment.

Paul's Experiences as Christ's Ambassador of Reconciliation

³We put no stumbling block in anyone's path, so that our ministry will not be discredited.

In his role as an ambassador of Christ Paul was well aware that he couldn't help the gospel achieve its purpose. That was the Holy Spirit's work. He could, however, hinder its effectiveness. One gospel-hindrance would be a lifestyle on the part of the ambassador that contradicted his message. Paul's concern was that he do nothing that might cast even the slightest shadow of doubt on the validity of the ministry of reconciliation. This is the context for understanding Paul's detailing of some of his experiences as Christ's ambassador in the verses that follow.

⁴Rather, as servants of God we commend ourselves in every way: in great endurance; in troubles, hardships and distresses; ⁵in beatings, imprisonments and riots; in hard work, sleepless nights and hunger;

Paul is not engaged in sinful boasting here. He feels compelled to review some of his activities as Christ's ambassador, to *commend* himself, for one reason only: what people see in the messenger may affect the credibility of his message.

Paul begins by listing some of the afflictions he experienced, all of which called for *great endurance*. He groups them by threes, beginning with three words that describe affliction in general: *troubles, hardships, and distresses.* In Acts 14:22 Paul had told the believers in Galatia, "We must go through many hardships to enter the kingdom of God." He had experienced many such troubles and hardships, many "tight squeezes" (as *distresses* could also be translated) where it appeared there would be no way out. But he did not back away from them.

He then lists three of the kinds of afflictions others inflicted on him: *beatings, imprisonments, and riots.* We think, for example, of how Paul was beaten and thrown into prison in Philippi (Acts 16) and of the riot in Ephesus (Acts 19). There were other such occasions, as is seen by the fact that all nine words in this listing are in the plural.

And finally, another list of three, this time what he allowed himself to endure: *hard work, sleepless nights, and hunger.* The word translated "hard work" could also be translated "toil." Paul grew weary in his labors. He also spent *sleepless nights.* Writing to the Thessalonians, he says, "We worked night and day" (2 Thessalonians 3:8), possibly a reference to missionary work by day and tent-making to support himself by night. He had refused to take any money from those among whom he worked. The result at times was *hunger.*

6in purity, understanding, patience and kindness; in the Holy Spirit and in sincere love; 7in truthful speech and in the power of God;

With these words, in two groups of fours, Paul reminds the Corinthians first of the attitude with which he carried out his ministry and then of the tools of his ministry. The first group of four consists of four single words: *in purity, understanding, patience, and kindness.* His motives were always pure as was his life and conduct. He sought always to be understanding, patient, and kind in his dealings with people.

The second group of four consists of two words each in the Greek: *in the Holy Spirit and in sincere love; in truthful speech and in the power of God.* The words translated "in the

Holy Spirit" would, it appears, be better translated with a small "h" and "s," thus making them a reference to the spirit with which Paul conducted his ministry. He did it in "a holy spirit and in sincere love," which distinguished him from the false, "super-apostles" whose spirit was anything but holy and whose "love" was hardly sincere.

With the words *in truthful speech and in the power of God* Paul shades over into the tools he used to carry out his ministry. *Truthful speech* is a possible translation, but it is better here to stick with a more literal translation: "the word of truth." Paul's ministry was carried out with the word, or message, of truth, which in Colossians 1:5 is specifically defined as the gospel. Notice how closely Paul ties in the phrase "the word of truth" with *the power of God,* as he does also in Romans 1:16, where he calls the gospel "the power of God for the salvation of everyone who believes."

There follows now a group of three at the end of verse seven into the beginning of verse eight, in which Paul expands on the subject of the tools of his ministry and comments on the persistence with which he carried on that ministry:

⁷with weapons of righteousness in the right hand and in the left; ⁸through glory and dishonor, bad report and good report.

He describes the "word of truth" which is the "power of God," as the *weapons of righteousness.* The "weapons of righteousness" are the powerful means by which the Holy Spirit conveys the righteousness of God won by Jesus (cf. 5:21) to people. He has conducted his ministry with the Spirit's sword, the Word of God, law and gospel, as his weapon so that the Corinthians' faith might not rest on Paul's wisdom, but on God's power (cf. Ephesians 6:17 and 1 Corinthians 2:5).

And he has not given up in the face of opposition. His ministry was at times accompanied with *glory,* as people accepted his message and as a result accorded honor to him as a true spokesman of God. At other times, however, it was accompanied with *dishonor.* Some rejected the gospel he brought and also treated the gospel-bearer with disrespect. Sometimes Paul's ministry met with *bad report.* Those who rejected his message spoke evil of the messenger. At other times his ministry met with *good report.* Those whom the Spirit led to accept his message had good things to say about the one who brought them that message.

Paul's point is that he had been consistent. He would not allow people's non-acceptance of the gospel to affect his ministry. He faithfully continued to use the word of truth, the Spirit's weapon for conveying to people the righteousness of Christ. People might stumble over the gospel. Paul had made sure that this stumbling would not occur because of what he had done or failed to do.

Finally, from the end of verse eight through verse ten, we see a series of seven terse antithetical statements. In each of these antitheses Paul is apparently contrasting the way his enemies were characterizing his ministry with what his ministry was really like.

genuine, yet regarded as impostors; [9]known, yet regarded as unknown; dying, and yet we live on; beaten, and yet not killed; [10]sorrowful, yet always rejoicing; poor, yet making many rich; having nothing, and yet possessing everything.

The Corinthians should recognize that things weren't always as they appeared on the surface. The opponents called Paul a deceiver, an *impostor;* in truth, he was a *genuine* apostle. They called him an *unknown,* a man without proper credentials; in truth, he was fully *known,* recognized as a true apostle both by God and by those who had benefitted from his ministry.

The unbelieving world sees only the negatives of the ministry. Paul's enemies undoubtedly capitalized on these negatives in their efforts to put him down in the eyes of the Corinthians. "Paul's a loser," they would say, "a weak man."

What would the world see when it looked at a man like Paul? It would see a man who appeared to be *dying.* Again and again he was just one step from death. It would see a man who was being *beaten,* literally, "chastised." It appeared as though, rather than being one of God's valued workers, God was constantly punishing him. The world would see a *sorrowful* man. It was with a sorrowful, heavy heart that Paul had visited Corinth prior to writing 1 Corinthians. And it was from a sorrowful, heavy heart that he had written much of that letter.

The world would see a man who was *poor,* barely keeping himself alive from day to day with his part-time tentmaking. The world, in fact, just looking at the surface of things, would probably describe a man like Paul as *having nothing.*

That's the world's view. The truth? *Dying, and yet we live on,* says Paul. In a previous chapter he had told the Corinthians, "We . . . are always being given over to death for Jesus' sake, so that his life may be revealed in our mortal body" (4:11). Paul *was beaten, but not yet killed.* The Lord had always rescued him. Several years later, in his final epistle, written shortly before his death, Paul confidently affirmed, "The Lord will rescue me from every evil attack and will bring me safely to his heavenly kingdom" (2 Timothy 4:18). That is exactly what happened.

Paul was *sorrowful, yet always rejoicing.* This joy was not a giddy public display of "happiness," but a deep joy in the

Lord which no negative outward circumstances could change. He was *poor, but making many rich.* To Paul the ministry didn't mean getting rich, but making others rich through the gospel. That he was constantly privileged to be doing.

The Paul whom the world characterized as *having nothing,* in reality could be described as *possessing everything.* That was because he had Christ. He needed nothing more, as he tells the Philippians, "Whatever was to my profit I now consider loss for the sake of Christ. . . . I consider everything a loss compared to the surpassing greatness of knowing Christ Jesus my Lord, for whose sake I have lost all things. I consider them rubbish, that I may gain Christ" (Philippians 3:7,8).

In these verses Paul's concern has not been for his own reputation. His concern has been for the reputation of the One who has called him into the ministry as an ambassador of reconciliation. In every way, Paul says, he has commended himself as a servant of God. The way he has conducted his ministry has been a credit, not a discredit, to Christ. Those who would say otherwise are guilty of deliberately falsifying the record, or at least of misinterpreting what they have seen.

One died for all. Through the work of that one Christ, God has reconciled the world to himself. Paul's actions as an ambassador of reconciliation have centered around getting that message out to the world. Hopefully, the Corinthians will understand and will turn away from anyone who would seek to drive a wedge between them and Paul.

THE MINISTRY OF THE NEW COVENANT
CALLS FOR SEPARATION
FROM UNBELIEVERS
(6:11-7:4)

A Plea for Closer Fellowship with Paul

11We have spoken freely to you, Corinthians, and opened wide our hearts to you.

All the way through this letter Paul has been dealing with an undercurrent of distrust and suspicion generated by those who opposed his ministry. Paul can't be trusted, they have charged. He says one thing and does another. One can't really know for sure what he means. Not to be able to trust Paul means not to be able to trust his message. And not to be able to trust his message means not to be sure of the reconciliation with God through Christ that was the heart of his message. That is why Paul has felt compelled to spend so much time defending his integrity.

Once again he returns to this same subject. One indicator of the depths of Paul's feelings about this matter is seen in the fact that he addresses his readers by name, *Corinthians*. On only two other occasions did Paul address by name in the body of his letter the ones to whom he was writing. Both times he was writing about a situation that had deeply moved him. He bemoaned the foolishness of the Galatians who were in danger of reverting to belief in salvation by works rather than by God's grace (Galatians 3:1), and he rejoiced over the generosity of the Philippians who alone of the churches Paul had founded had given him financial assistance (Philippians 4:15).

Here in 2 Corinthians Paul's urgent concern is that the Corinthians take him at his word. He says, *We have spoken freely to you, Corinthians,* literally, "We have opened our mouths to you." Sometimes what comes out of a person's mouth is not a good indicator of what the person is really thinking. He says one thing but means something else. Paul wants the Corinthians to be sure that such is not the case with him. What has come out of his mouth has proceeded directly from his heart: *We have . . . opened wide our hearts to you.* There was no contradiction between mouth and heart, between what Paul said and what Paul meant. His words expressed the feelings of his heart. He had held nothing back from the Corinthians. There was no hidden agenda.

12We are not withholding our affection from you, but you are withholding yours from us. 13As a fair exchange — I speak as to my children — open wide your hearts also.

Paul had been open and forthright with the Corinthians. Why, then, had tensions and suspicions begun to mar the fine relationship they had enjoyed with each other? The problem, Paul says, lay with the Corinthians who apparently were listening too uncritically to those who opposed Paul's ministry in Corinth.

Paul asserts that he was not *withholding* his *affection* from the Corinthians. The problem was the other way around: They were withholding their affection from Paul. The word which the NIV translates as "withholding affection" has in it the idea of putting something into a narrow, cramped space. We might paraphrase Paul's words this way: "It's not that we don't have room for you Corinthians in our hearts, but rather that you don't have room for us." It's not that Paul hadn't been open with the Corinthians. The problem is that the Corinthians were not opening up their hearts to Paul.

It shouldn't be that way. Paul, as the spiritual father of the believers in Corinth, felt deeply for them as his *children.* His heart went out to them. Now, *as a fair exchange,* they should treat Paul in the same way. He pleads, *Open wide your hearts also.* It is only right, only natural, in fact, that the Corinthians should treat Paul, their spiritual father, in the same way that he was treating them as his spiritual children.

The horizontal fellowship Christians enjoy, their fellowship with one another as God's redeemed children, is a marvelous blessing of God. This fellowship reveals itself in ways such as Paul has mentioned in these verses: We are open and transparent with each other. We have much room in our hearts for one another. We trust one another.

The fact that such isn't always the case is a reminder that Satan is still at work in Christians, operating through the old sinful nature. He longs to destroy this fellowship through which Christians can help and strengthen each other. He works to cause Christians to revert to the way the heathen act, "being hated and hating one another" (Titus 3:3). Perhaps we, too, along with the Corinthians, need the reminder not to withhold our affections but rather to open wide our hearts to one another. We need each other, just as the Corinthians needed Paul and Paul needed the Corinthians.

A Warning against Fellowship with Unbelievers

14Do not be yoked together with unbelievers.

With these words Paul is bringing out another reason why the Corinthians should reaffirm their close fellowship ties with Paul. By turning away from Paul and toward Paul's opponents, not only were they losing out on some of the blessings of Christian fellowship, but they were actually fellowshiping with unbelief. This wasn't merely something they were coming close to doing. It was already occurring, as a more literal translation of the command, *Do not be yoked together with unbelievers,* makes clear. Paul is telling the Corinthians, "Stop being yoked together with unbelievers."

Paul doesn't identify the false beliefs of those unbelieving teachers who were opposing him. He makes it clear, however, that when he urges the Corinthians to turn away from these people and to adhere more closely to him, it is not Paul's wounded pride talking. It is not so much that the Corinthians' action is hurting Paul as it is hurting the Corinthians themselves. If they opened up their hearts to these false teachers instead of to Paul, this would be destructive to their faith.

Paul therefore urges them, "Stop being yoked together with unbelievers." There is a similar verse in the law of Moses: "Do not plow with an ox and a donkey yoked together" (Deuteronomy 22:10). According to God's law the ox was a clean animal while the donkey was unclean. The two should not be yoked together. So it is with believer and unbeliever. For them to be joined together would be a mismating. They are totally incompatible with one another.

Paul's point is not that believer and unbeliever dare never have any contact with each other. "In that case," as Paul had written earlier in 1 Corinthians, "you would have to leave the world" (1 Corinthians 5:10). Christ's commission to his church to make disciples of all nations could hardly be carried out if believers were called upon to totally avoid unbelievers. Paul's directive, *Do not be yoked together with unbelievers,* refers rather to a spiritual "yoking," or fellowship. The

Corinthian believers are to avoid any association with unbelievers — such as these false teachers — that would compromise their faith.

With five rhetorical questions Paul drives home this "Don't be yoked together with unbelievers" principle:

For what do righteousness and wickedness have in common? Or what fellowship can light have with darkness? ¹⁵What harmony is there between Christ and Belial? What does a believer have in common with an unbeliever? ¹⁶What agreement is there between the temple of God and idols? For we are the temple of the living God. As God has said: "I will live with them and walk among them, and I will be their God, and they will be my people."

The answer to each of these questions is the same, isn't it? Nothing! None! *Righteousness and wickedness* have nothing in common. Clothed in the garments of Christ's holiness, Christians have become "the righteousness of God" (2 Corinthians 5:21), while unbelievers in God's eyes are totally "workers of wickedness" (cf. Matthew 7:23). They have nothing in common.

What fellowship can light have with darkness? Again, the answer is obvious. Christ is the Light of the world (John 8:12). Christians belong to Christ and share in his light. They have been called out of darkness into light (1 Peter 2:9). They now are light in the Lord (Ephesians 5:8). One cannot be both light and darkness at the same time.

What harmony is there between Christ and Belial, that is, Satan? Christ came into the world to destroy the works of the devil (1 John 3:8). How foolish, then, to try to walk with both Christ and Satan. But that is exactly what one is doing if the Christian, who belongs to Christ, extends the hand of fellowship to the unbeliever, who belongs to Satan.

What does a believer have in common with an unbeliever?
Ultimately, the unbeliever's life centers around self; the believers' life centers around Christ. How can they, therefore, be yoked together? They are pulling in different directions.

What agreement is there between the temple of God and idols? In his first letter, Paul had reminded the Corinthians, "Your body is a temple of the Holy Spirit. . . . You are not your own; you were bought at a price" (1 Corinthians 6:19,20). How could they now be opening up their hearts to false teachers? The same heart cannot be a home for both the true God and for idols.

Only one course of action is called for:

17"Therefore come out from them and be separate, says the Lord. Touch no unclean thing, and I will receive you." 18"I will be a Father to you, and you will be my sons and daughters, says the Lord Almighty."

At the beginning of this section Paul had put it negatively, *Do not be yoked together with unbelievers.* Now he says it positively, *Come out from among them and be separate.* He is freely quoting here a number of verses from the Old Testament, in that way making it clear that this had always been God's will. God's people, the children of Israel, were not to fellowship with the unbelievers in whose midst they lived. So the Corinthian Christians, a part of God's new Israel, his *sons and daughters* in Christ, should not forfeit the blessings of true fellowship by allowing themselves to be mis-mated with unbelievers.

7 **Since we have these promises, dear friends, let us purify ourselves from everything that contaminates body and spirit, perfecting holiness out of reverence for God.**

The *promises* Paul is speaking of are those he has just referred to at the end of verse 16 and in verse 18: "I will live with them and walk among them, and I will be their God, and they will be my people. . . . I will be a Father to you, and you will be my sons and daughters." One can't have anything better than that: fellowship with God and through that fellowship with God's people. The Corinthians will want to cleanse themselves of false fellowships, which pollute, *contaminate,* rather than enrich the lives of God's sons and daughters.

Paul urges them to be *perfecting holiness out of reverence for God.* The word translated holiness is often also translated "sanctification," while the word translated *perfecting* has in it the idea of reaching a goal. Paul wants the Corinthians to be striving for continued growth in their life of sanctification — in the matter of their fellowship relations also. They shouldn't revert to their former state by joining themselves with false teachers.

Before moving on, we should mention that there are some who contend that these words, *Do not be yoked together with unbelievers,* find a specific application in one's choice of a marriage partner. The contention is that Paul here is forbidding a Christian to marry a non-Christian, for that would be joining righteousness and wickedness, light and darkness.

While it is true that many difficulties and dangers attach themselves to the marriage of a believer to an unbeliever, this passage can hardly be used to support a prohibition of such marriages. Paul is talking about a *spiritual* yoking of believer and unbeliever, the kind of false fellowship the Corinthians had allowed themselves to enter by joining hands with the false teachers who opposed Paul. Marriage in and of itself is not a spiritual union, and therefore, we can safely say, was not what Paul was aiming at as he wrote these words.

This is not to say, of course, that one should not warn Christians about the pitfalls of a Christian/non-Christian marriage, for the best foundation on which to build a marriage is on the solid rock of a common faith in Jesus Christ. It is just to say that this passage should not be used as an absolute prohibition of believer-unbeliever marriages, since that is not the subject Paul is talking about.

The Plea for Closer Fellowship Repeated

²Make room for us in your hearts. We have wronged no one, we have corrupted no one, we have exploited no one. ³I do not say this to condemn you; I have said before that you have such a place in our hearts that we would live or die with you.

After his strong warning against fellowship with unbelievers, Paul returns to the thought of chapter 6:11-13. When he says, *Make room for us,* he uses a form of the same word he used in 6:12 where he admonished the Corinthians for "withholding" their "affection" from Paul. They had squeezed Paul out of their lives. They no longer had room for him. Now he urges them, *Make room for us.*

There is no reason why the believers in Corinth should not again make room for Paul in their hearts. Without any qualification Paul can assert, *We have wronged no one, we have corrupted no one, we have exploited no one.* Each of these is a deliberate understatement. Not only had Paul not wronged the Corinthians, he had done them the greatest good by bringing them the good news of Jesus Christ. Not only had Paul not corrupted the Corinthians, he had lifted them up from the mire of corruption and decay into the new life that is in Christ. Not only had Paul not greedily exploited the Corinthians, he had not accepted so much as a penny from them, even though he had the right to do so.

I do not say this to condemn you, he tells them. He has not been admonishing the Corinthians because he finds delight in putting them down. He does it because he loves them. He has already said that his heart was wide open to them (cf. 6:11), and now he repeats that thought and adds to it: *You have such a place in our hearts that we would live or die with you.*

The NIV translation reverses the order of the end of this sentence. As it stands in the original Greek, the passage reads, "You are in our hearts to die with you and to keep on living with you." We cannot be altogether sure of what Paul means when he talks about dying with the Corinthians and continuing to live with them. We are perhaps given a clue in another of Paul's letters, where he writes, "If we died with him [that is, Christ], we will also live with him" (2 Timothy 2:11). In that verse he is talking about the Christian's fellowship with Christ, which begins with "death," as one is buried with Christ in baptism and then continues in a brand new life as Christ's brother or sister. In the verse before us, Paul could well be referring to the same thing. The emphasis here, however, is on the mutual fellowship in Christ he and the Corinthians enjoyed. In Christ both had "died" and become new people and now were joined together to live as brothers and sisters of Jesus — a life that would continue into eternity. You cannot have any closer relationship than that!

⁴I have great confidence in you; I take great pride in you. I am greatly encouraged; in all our troubles my joy knows no bounds.

With these words Paul is beginning to move back to the thought which he had interrupted several chapters ago (cf. 2:12-13). Paul had sent Titus ahead of him to Corinth to see how the Corinthians had responded to the strongly worded letter we today call 1 Corinthians. So anxious had Paul been to receive word from Titus, that when he traveled north to meet him in Troas and didn't find him there, he kept on moving in the direction of Corinth. Even though the Lord had "opened a door" (2:12) for mission work in Troas, Paul didn't step through that door. Because of his concern about the Corinthians, he couldn't concentrate on anything else. He wrote, "I still had no peace of mind, because I did not find my brother Titus there [in Troas]. So I said good-by to them and went on to Macedonia" (2:13).

Then came the long "digression" (2:14-7:4), forming the major part of the first section of 2 Corinthians, in which Paul extolled the praises of the ministry of the New Covenant — a ministry that surpasses the ministry of the Old Covenant, a ministry entrusted to fragile jars of clay, a ministry of universal reconciliation, a ministry that calls for separation from those who by unbelief would rob this ministry of its full luster.

Now Paul's thoughts return to the mission of Titus. When Paul finally met up with him, what did Titus tell him about the Corinthians? Paul will be speaking directly to that subject in the verses that follow, but he tips his hand a little even before doing so. He says of the Corinthians, *I have great confidence in you.* Translated a bit more literally, Paul is saying, "Great is my boldness, my frankness, toward you." "I know," he says, "that I have had to speak in a rather forcible way to your face." But at the same time Paul can say, *I take great pride in you.* "I am optimistic about you," Paul says. *I am greatly encouraged; in all our troubles my joy knows no bounds.* He then reveals why he can talk that way, why, even with all the problems in Corinth, his joy is overflowing: Titus has come back with some very good news.

PAUL'S JOYFUL REUNION WITH TITUS
(7:5-16)

Good News from Titus

**⁵For when we came into Macedonia, this body of ours had
no rest, but we were harassed at every turn — conflicts on the
outside, fears within.**

After a three-year stay in Ephesus, at the close of what we
today call the third missionary journey, Paul had traveled
north to Troas to meet Titus. Titus had gone ahead of Paul to
Corinth, apparently with the understanding that once he had
ascertained how things were going there he would travel to
Troas, meet Paul, and tell him what he had discovered. Not
finding Titus in Troas, Paul had crossed the Aegean Sea and
come to the province of Macedonia, hoping to meet him
there. In Macedonia, he says, *This body of ours had no rest.*
Things were no better for Paul there than they had been in
Troas because Titus was still not to be found. Paul tells the
Corinthians, *We were harassed at every turn — conflicts on
the outside, fears within.* He is probably talking about the
great anguish of spirit he was suffering as he waited for Titus
to arrive with news from Corinth.

We should not fail to note here the depths of feeling Paul
had for the Christians in Corinth. That congregation had
probably caused him more sleepless nights than any of those
he had founded. It was in many ways his "problem child."
He could have adopted a cynical "they've made their bed;

116

now let them lie in it" attitude toward the Corinthians. We see just the opposite, however. They were constantly on his mind and in his heart. He longed to do what he could to help them.

As shepherds of flocks and elders in the church today work with what are sometimes called "delinquent" members, they could hardly find a better role model than Paul. The temptation might be to become cynical, to write off too quickly the possibility of restoring straying sinners to the right path. The Pauline approach is to keep such people in our hearts, to feel for them deeply, to care for them intensely, not to give up on them until we have exhausted every possible avenue to win them back.

6But God, who comforts the downcast, comforted us by the coming of Titus, 7and not only by his coming but also by the comfort you had given him. He told us about your longing for me, your deep sorrow, your ardent concern for me, so that my joy was greater than ever.

A dominant note in this epistle is that of comfort and encouragement. Right after his greeting to the Corinthians, Paul had written, "Praise be to the God and Father of our Lord Jesus Christ, the Father of compassion and the God of all *comfort,* who *comforts* us in all our troubles, so that we can *comfort* those in any trouble with the *comfort* we ourselves have received from God" (1:3,4).

God *comforts* and encourages his people directly through the many promises in his word. He also brings them comfort and encouragement through fellow believers. That is the kind of *comfort* Paul is talking about here. It revolves around his meeting with Titus and the report Titus brought about the situation in Corinth.

117

Paul was comforted and encouraged in three ways. First, he says, *God . . . comforted us by the coming of Titus*. The arrival of Titus in Macedonia, considerably later, apparently, than the previously agreed upon meeting time, was itself a source of comfort to Paul. We can imagine the kinds of thoughts that ran through Paul's mind as he anxiously waited for Titus. Was he meeting with such difficulty in Corinth that it was taking him much longer than planned to get things settled? Had he perhaps become ill? Had he encountered some problems along the way? Had he been struck down by bandits who had pounced upon this lone traveler? Had he perhaps been killed? Parents whose college-attending son or daughter is hours late on a wintry night in returning home from school at vacation time understand these kinds of feelings.

Parents also understand how just seeing the face of Titus provided instant relief to Paul. Their child might return home with news about a break-down of some kind or a minor accident along the way. But for the time being that would not be the most important thing. Their son or daughter whom they love is home. That is what counts above all. So it was with Paul, who dearly loved Titus. Even if Titus had bad news to report, at least this much was good: Titus was alive and well. That was great comfort to Paul.

Paul, however, was comforted in a second way. Not just the arrival of Titus, but also the report of Titus was a source of great encouragement to Paul. Titus had some good news to relate. Paul summarizes the report of Titus in three phrases. First of all, Paul tells the Corinthians, Titus *told us about your longing for me*. They had a fervent desire to see Paul again. After the stern words Paul had felt compelled to write in 1 Corinthians, it was not at all certain they would even consent to see Paul again, much less long to see him. That was great news for Paul, not so much for what that meant to him personally but for what it implied about the Corinthians. A longing to see Paul again also meant a longing to continue to hear the message Paul had brought to them.

Secondly, Paul says, Titus told me about *your deep sorrow.* This is most likely a reference to sorrow over the sins they had committed or had condoned in others. Paul could be thinking in particular about the case of incest which they had allowed to continue without disciplinary action (cf. 1 Corinthians 5:1-5).

How such sorrow over sin is good news Paul will discuss in the verses that follow. But first he relates a third aspect of the report of Titus. Titus, Paul tells the Corinthians, told me of *your ardent concern for me.* How this ardent concern manifested itself among the Corinthians is also the subject of the next verses.

Even without going into the detail that follows, however, one can see how Paul can exclaim that as a result of Titus' report his *joy was greater than ever.* The Corinthians longed to see Paul; they were sorry for what they had done to disrupt their close fellowship with Paul; they were ardently concerned for Paul, once again zealous to hear, accept, and put into practice the message that he, the Lord's spokesman, had brought to them.

8Even if I caused you sorrow by my letter, I do not regret it. Though I did regret it — I see that my letter hurt you, but only for a little while — 9yet now I am happy, not because you were made sorry, but because your sorrow led you to repentance. For you became sorrowful as God intended and so were not harmed in any way by us. 10Godly sorrow brings repentance that leads to salvation and leaves no regret, but worldly sorrow brings death.

What is the letter Paul is referring to here? As discussed earlier, we are proceeding on the assumption that the reference is to the letter we today call 1 Corinthians. During his third missionary journey, Paul, while in Ephesus, had paid a visit to Corinth. This was a "painful" visit because he had to speak quite sternly about some of the godless ways being tolerated there, in particular the undisciplined case of incest (2 Corinthians 2:1). Following this visit, Paul had written a letter to the congregation in Corinth "out of great distress and anguish of heart and with many tears" (2 Corinthians 2:4). That letter, it appears quite certain, was 1 Corinthians and is the same letter referred to in the verse before us (cf. the exposition of 2:1-4 for the rationale behind this assumption).

This letter, 1 Corinthians, had caused *sorrow;* grief, to the Corinthians. It was not easy to listen to the kind of stern rebuke Paul had felt compelled to issue in 1 Corinthians. Nor was it easy for Paul to write such a letter. Yet, says Paul, *I do not regret it.*

But in the next breath Paul adds, *Though I did regret it.* With these words Paul is not demonstrating inconsistency. He is simply telling it like it is. Any parent who has been compelled to discipline a child easily grasps what Paul means. No one likes to inflict anything painful on one he loves. If that, however, is the only course of action which will produce the proper results, then the loving parent does it, all the while regretting that he or she has to cause a loved one to suffer pain of any kind.

I see that my letter hurt you, caused you to grieve, says Paul. That is what he regrets, but, he notes, this grief was *only for a little while.* The grief was meant to be only temporary. Sorrow over sin was intended to be replaced by the joy of forgiveness.

And that is exactly what had happened. That is why Paul can say, *Now I am happy.* He is happy, he tells the Corinthians, *Not because you were made sorry, but because your sorrow led you to repentance.* There is a difference, isn't there? Only a sadistic person takes pleasure in making someone unhappy. If, however, one uses the sharp edge of the law to cut deeply into a person's conscience, not to hurt him but to lead him to a knowledge of his sin and to repentance, that is a different story. That, says Paul, is sorrow *as God intended,* sorrow that does not harm, but rather helps, the sinner.

Paul calls it *godly* sorrow. *Godly sorrow brings repentance that leads to salvation.* This is the kind of sorrow Titus had seen in the Corinthians. Paul contrasts this godly sorrow with *worldly* sorrow. Worldly sorrow is the kind of sorrow that, for example, Judas displayed after he betrayed Jesus. He was sorry that he had done it, but that was all. Such sorrow *brings death.* It results in eternal sorrow, in weeping and gnashing of teeth that will never end (cf. Matthew 25:30).

Paul now points to evidence that the Corinthians' sorrow was of the godly, not the worldly, variety:

11See what this godly sorrow has produced in you: what earnestness, what eagerness to clear yourselves, what indignation, what alarm, what longing, what concern, what readiness to see justice done. At every point you have proved yourselves to be innocent in this matter.

The Corinthians were displaying a real *earnestness,* just the opposite of their former broad-minded, complacent attitude, which had indifferently shrugged its shoulders even at a case of incest within the congregation. Now they were taking the matter seriously.

There was now *an eagerness to clear* themselves of being involved in the sin of another by failing to take proper disciplinary action. There was *indignation,* a feeling of revulsion against the sin they had allowed to go unchecked before. There was *alarm,* literally "fear," a renewed humble reverence for the word of the Lord as spoken by his chosen apostle, Paul. There was *longing,* which Paul had already referred to (verse 7), a longing to see Paul once again. There was *concern,* a zeal to do all things in the way they should be done.

All of these godly attitudes were evidenced in their *readiness to see justice done.* In 1 Corinthians, Paul had exhorted them, "Hand this man [the one guilty of an ongoing incestuous relationship] over to Satan, so that the sinful nature may be destroyed and his spirit saved on the day of the Lord" (1 Corinthians 5:5). That they had done. Paul, therefore, can say with joy, *At every point you have proved yourselves to be innocent in the matter.* The guilt of failing to do what had to be done no longer rested on their shoulders. They had listened to Paul's loving rebuke, were filled with sorrow over their sin, and had repented. The fruit of their repentance was the action they had taken with this man.

That the welfare of the whole congregation was in Paul's mind when he wrote about the man who needed to be disciplined is clear from what follows.

12So even though I wrote to you, it was not on account of the one who did the wrong or of the injured party, but rather that before God you could see for yourselves how devoted to us you are. 13By all this we are encouraged.

Paul is most likely referring once again to 1 Corinthians 5. The *one who did the wrong* would be the man guilty of the sin of incest. The *injured party* would be his father. Paul says that he hadn't written to the Corinthians on account of them. Not that he was unconcerned about these individuals — the sin of the one and the anguish and pain of the other, but rather that he had a broader concern in writing. He wanted his words to set the whole congregation in Corinth back on the right track, particularly in its relationship with him.

His intent was that the Corinthians come to realize once again that Paul was their spiritual father and a preacher of the true gospel, the one who really loved them. His hope was that as a result of his letter (1 Corinthians) they would treasure even more deeply the presence and work of Paul.

The prayer of Paul's heart was that, as the Corinthians listened to and responded to his words, they would come to see how *devoted to* [literally, "zealous for"] Paul they actually were and, by way of contrast, how little the false teachers merited any consideration. It appears as though Paul's prayer had been answered. By this, he says, he was *encouraged.*

In this whole section Paul has been talking about the spiritual benefit that comes from disciplining erring Christians. We today need to listen carefully to these words. There is sometimes a hesitancy among God's people, both in the home and in the church, to discipline those who have gone astray. Parents don't like to "hurt" their children or they fear a negative reaction. The same can happen in the church.

The words of Paul in the verses above remind us that if we really love a person, we will not hesitate to practice loving discipline. We will use the law to reveal sin, even though it may hurt for a little while, for we know that without knowledge of sin there is no sorrow over sin or repentance. Without repentance there is no forgiveness. Without forgiveness there is no salvation. On the other hand, use of the law as mirror to reveal sin leads, as Paul says, to "godly sorrow." And "godly sorrow brings repentance that leads to salvation" (2 Corinthians 7:10).

Paul's Joy for Titus' Sake

We said above that with the arrival of Titus, Paul was comforted and encouraged in three ways. We have looked at two of these three ways. First, Paul drew great comfort from the very fact of Titus' arrival (verse 6). Secondly, Paul was much encouraged through the report Titus gave about the improved situation in Corinth (verses 7-12). Now in the closing verses of this chapter Paul mentions a third way he was encouraged: when he heard of the warm reception the Corinthians had given to Titus.

In addition to our own encouragement, we were especially delighted to see how happy Titus was, because his spirit has been refreshed by all of you. ¹⁴I had boasted to him about you, and you have not embarrassed me. But just as everything we said to you was true, so our boasting about you to Titus has proved to be true as well.

The spirit of Titus *has been refreshed,* says Paul. He uses here a form of the Greek verb which indicates that this was still true about Titus. At the time when Paul was writing this letter, the effects of the warm reception given him by the Corinthians still hadn't worn off. Moreover, it wasn't just a few of the Corinthians who had shown kindness to Titus. Paul says that the spirit of Titus had been refreshed by *all* of the Corinthians.

I had boasted to him about you, Paul tells them. He had evidently assured Titus as he left for Corinth that, though the problems there were deep and many, the Corinthians were children of God. Titus, therefore, could be sure they would welcome him properly and would respond to his admonitions. And that is exactly what had happened. *You have not embarrassed me,* says Paul, which they would have done if they had given Titus a cool reception or even refused to receive him.

The fact that what Paul told Titus about the Corinthians proved to be true was consistent with Paul's whole ministry among the Corinthians. *Everything we said to you was true,* he reminds them; so it should come as no surprise that what he said to Titus about the Corinthians *proved to be true as well.* With these words, as he draws close to the end of the first major section of 2 Corinthians, Paul one more time drives home the point that the Corinthians can trust him in all that he says. As he had insisted earlier in the letter, what comes out of his mouth is not "Yes" and "No" (1:18). He speaks only the truth.

15And his affection for you is all the greater when he remembers that you were all obedient, receiving him with fear and trembling. 16I am glad I can have complete confidence in you.

It wasn't just the kind way in which the Corinthians had welcomed him that had refreshed the spirit of Titus. Even more important was the way they had received his message. The Corinthians were *obedient.* Paul is referring here to what he calls elsewhere the "obedience of faith." The Corinthians accepted what Titus said as the very word of God.

That is why they had received Titus *with fear and trembling.* They respected him as a man of God who was bringing into their midst the very word of God. This was a welcome about-face from the contemptuous attitude that at least some of them had begun to display toward Paul.

The first major section of 2 Corinthians thus ends on a high note. Paul says, *I am glad I can have complete confidence in you.* The NIV translation weakens the original language somewhat. The word "can" is not in the Greek. Paul's concluding statement before he proceeds to a different subject is, more literally translated, "I have confidence in you in every way."

He doesn't mean there are no more hurdles to be crossed. In the next two chapters he is going to bring up the subject of the offering for the church in Jerusalem which the Corinthians have yet to complete. And in the final chapters he will once again feel compelled to take aim at the "super-apostles" who are trying to disrupt the fellowship between Paul and the Corinthians. Paul, however, could approach both of these issues in the confidence that the Corinthians truly desired to believe and do what God says, that they still looked to Paul as their spiritual father, and that they were ready to receive Paul's message as the very word of God. What more could he expect!

So it is that with joy Paul brings to a close the first major portion of 2 Corinthians. In 2 Corinthians 1-7 he has looked to the past. He has explained his change in itinerary at the close of his third missionary journey, which his detractors have used to charge him with being untrustworthy. In the process he has extolled in language unequalled in Scripture the glory of the ministry of the new covenant.

PART TWO:
A LOOK TO THE PRESENT —
PAUL URGES COMPLETION OF
THE OFFERING FOR THE CHURCH
AT JERUSALEM
(8:1-9:15)

The two chapters that follow form the lengthiest discussion on the subject of Christian stewardship in the Scriptures. Paul's words were occasioned by a specific situation: an offering for needy believers in Jerusalem which was being gathered by the churches in the provinces of Galatia, Asia, Macedonia, and Achaia.

From quite an early date, the Jews in Jerusalem who had accepted Jesus of Nazareth as the Messiah had to contend with poverty. At times the poverty was brought on by natural causes. Acts 11 speaks of a severe famine which prompted the believers in Antioch of Syria "to provide help for the brothers living in Judea" (Acts 11:29). Paul was one of the two who had brought financial aid from Antioch to Judea.

Another cause of poverty may well have stemmed from persecution. It would not have been a popular move in Jerusalem to publicly identify oneself as a follower of Jesus Christ. It is, therefore, not unreasonable to suppose that believing Jews would be ostracized from the rest of the Jewish community, making it difficult for them to earn a living.

At any rate, poverty seemed to be a major problem among the believers in Jerusalem. Some years before the writing of

"Though he was rich, yet for your sakes he became poor."

2 Corinthians, in fact, the leaders of the church in Jerusalem had petitioned the apostles to the Gentiles, Paul and Barnabas, to continue to remember their poor brothers and sisters in Jerusalem. That, Paul said, was "the very thing I was eager to do" (Galatians 2:10).

The offering he was gathering from the churches in Galatia, Asia, Macedonia, and Achaia is an example of Paul's eagerness to continue to be helpful in a material way to the less well-off church in Jerusalem.

The book of Acts makes only a brief mention of this particular relief offering (Acts 24:17), so we must look to Paul's letters to try to piece together some details. It is mentioned in three places: here in 2 Corinthians 8 and 9, in 1 Corinthians 16:1-4, and in Romans 15:25-28. From these references we can ascertain that Paul looked upon the offering as a tangible way of expressing the oneness in Christ that Jew and Gentile Christians shared, as well as a way of repaying the debt of love the Gentile believers owed to the Jewish believers. As Paul wrote to the Romans, "If the Gentiles have shared in the Jews' spiritual blessings, they owe it to the Jews to share with them their material blessings" (Romans 15:27).

The intention, it appears, was that representatives from the various churches involved in the offering, perhaps along with Paul, would travel to Jerusalem and personally present this gift to their fellow Christians. In 1 Corinthians 16 Paul had given some specific instructions on how this offering should be gathered. The people should be setting aside some funds on a regular, systematic basis. Then, when Paul arrived, it would be ready to go (cf. 1 Corinthians 16:1-4).

As Paul brings out in the section of 2 Corinthians before us, the Corinthian congregation had been an eager participant in this offering and had started out well. But then things began to lag. All of the problems in Corinth could well have been the cause of the disruption in the gathering of the offering. At any rate, Paul was soon going to arrive in Corinth, and the Corinthians were not ready. A main purpose in writing about the offering in 2 Corinthians was to encourage the Corinthians, as he put it, "to finish the work, so that your eager willingness to do it may be matched by your completion of it" (2 Corinthians 8:11).

ENCOURAGEMENT TO COMPLETE
THE OFFERING
(8:1-15)

The Example of the Macedonians

8 **And now, brothers, we want you to know about the grace that God has given the Macedonian churches. ²Out of the most severe trial, their overflowing joy and their extreme poverty welled up in rich generosity.**

Paul addresses the Corinthians as *brothers,* that is, fellow believers. The report from Titus had made it clear that they had not abandoned Paul or the gospel he had brought to them. He could, therefore, begin to talk about the subject of giving, confident that the Corinthians, as members of the family of God, desired to do what was pleasing to the Lord also in this area of Christian living.

He begins by using the churches in the province of Macedonia as an example. Macedonia was just to the north of the province of Achaia, where Corinth was located. Paul had done mission work in three cities in Macedonia: Philippi, Thessalonica, and Berea (cf. Acts 16:11-17:14).

The Philippians in particular had demonstrated great generosity toward Paul. Writing to the congregation in Philippi,

Paul reminds them of the way they had come to his assistance after he had left Philippi: "When I was in Thessalonica, you sent me aid again and again when I was in need" (Philippians 4:16). Later, when Paul was a prisoner in Rome, the Philippians sent a personal representative, Epaphroditus, all the way to Rome with gifts from the church, gifts that Paul calls "a fragrant offering, an acceptable sacrifice, pleasing to God" (Philippians 4:18).

The congregation in Philippi as well as those in Thessalonica and Berea had been no less generous when it came to the offering for the Jerusalem church. Looking at the situation these believers were in, one would probably not have predicted such a response. Paul reports that they gave this offering *out of the most severe trial*. Evidently these churches were encountering stiff opposition. They were being persecuted. And they were extremely poor. Humanly speaking, persecution and poverty were hardly the raw material for generous offerings.

But that did not deter the Macedonians. In their severe trial they continued to experience *overflowing joy*. The believers in Macedonia understood what Martin Luther was to say many years later: "And take they our life, goods, fame, child, and wife, let these all be gone, they yet have nothing won; the Kingdom ours remaineth (TLH 262:4)." No persecution, however severe, could rob them of the joy of salvation.

That joy *welled up in rich generosity* in the midst of their *extreme poverty*. Their poverty no more hampered their generosity than their persecution hindered their joy. The word translated "generosity" in the NIV will be used by Paul elsewhere in 2 Corinthians 8 and 9. It is worth a closer look. It comes from a word with the root meaning of "single"; its basic idea is that of "singleness, or single-mindedness, of purpose." Thus it points more to the attitude of the giver than it does to the amount given.

It is the same word Paul uses in Romans 12:8 where he talks about the special spiritual gift of "contributing to the needs of others." If one has that gift, says Paul, then let him give "generously," that is, with single-mindedness of purpose, without any ulterior, self-serving motives.

So it was with the believers in Macedonia. Though they were living in abject poverty, their joy in the Lord moved them to give from that poverty when they were apprised of the plight of their sisters and brothers in Jerusalem. They could not help but give. Their *overflowing joy and their extreme poverty welled up in rich generosity.*

We should also note the ultimate source of this single-minded, generous spirit. In the opening verse of this section Paul attributes it to *the grace that God has given* to the churches in Macedonia. Generous givers aren't born that way; such an attitude is a result of being re-born. The grace, or unmerited love, of God that brings salvation to the sinner also inspires a new life of service that includes unselfish, generous giving.

In the verses that follow Paul gives three examples of the single-minded, generous giving of the Macedonian Christians:

3For I testify that they gave as much as they were able, and even beyond their ability. Entirely on their own, 4they urgently pleaded with us for the privilege of sharing in this service to the saints. 5And they did not do as we expected, but they gave themselves first to the Lord and then to us in keeping with God's will.

First, the believers in the churches in Macedonia had given not just as much as they could but even more than that. The poor widow and her "mite" come to mind. With the widow, the Macedonians too had been what some might term reckless in their giving. They had given more than some people might have considered to be wise and prudent.

Secondly, no one had pressured them into giving. They had decided *entirely on their own* to be so overwhelmingly generous in their offering. They had, in fact, begged, *urgently pleaded,* Paul says, to be included in the offering. How many churches today, how many individual Christians, fit into the category of those whose longing to give an offering is so great that they won't take "No" for an answer?

The Macedonians considered it a privilege, a gift of God's grace, that they could be part of this offering. Paul calls the offering a *sharing in . . . service to the saints.* The word translated "sharing" is the same word that elsewhere is translated "fellowship." It has in it the idea of a oneness, a unity, a having things in common. The Christians in Macedonia were expressing their fellowship, their unity in Christ, with the Christians in Jerusalem through this offering.

The word translated "service" could also be translated "ministry." Christians minister to one another, they serve one another, as they give offerings to help their fellow *saints,* that is, believers, in their spiritual or physical needs.

A third example of the God-granted single-minded attitude of the Macedonians is found in verse 5. The Macedonians gave even more than an offering of money; they gave themselves. In the original Greek the word *themselves* is placed in an emphatic position. Paul says, *Themselves they gave first to the Lord and then to us.*

In a few months Paul would be writing a letter to the church at Rome. In that letter, after reviewing for the Christians at Rome God's marvelous plan of salvation, Paul says by way of application, "Therefore, I urge you, brothers, in view of God's mercy, to offer your bodies as living sacrifices, holy and pleasing to God" (Romans 12:1). That is precisely what the Christians in Macedonia had done. They had offered back their whole selves to the Lord who had offered his Son into death for them. Along with this offering of self had come the offering of their treasures.

In the matter of giving, is it right to hold up to Christians the example of other Christians? Paul certainly does just that. Modeling is an important factor in helping Christians learn how they might use their money. We should not fail to note, however, the way Paul uses other Christians as models. His emphasis is not on the amount they are giving, but on the attitude they are displaying, an attitude which looks upon giving as a privilege, an attitude that requires no prompting to give, an attitude that says, "I give myself, and that includes my offerings, as a thank-offering to my Lord who gave himself first for me." That, Paul says, is an example worth emulating.

The Example of the Corinthians Themselves

6So we urged Titus, since he had earlier made a beginning, to bring also to completion this act of grace on your part. 7But just as you excel in everything — in faith, in speech, in knowledge, in complete earnestness and in your love for us — see that you also excel in this grace of giving.

This is the third reference to Titus in 2 Corinthians. For background on what we know about Titus, the reader can refer to the exposition of 2:13. When had Titus *made a beginning* of this offering? The opening words of 1 Corinthians 16, "Now about the collection for God's people," assume that the Corinthians already at that time had some acquaintance with the offering. Evidently, therefore, Titus had visited

Corinth some time before the writing of 1 Corinthians. The visit would have taken place about one year before the writing of 2 Corinthians (cf. 2 Corinthians 9:2), and thus would have occurred while Paul was in Ephesus on his third missionary journey. Now Paul wants to send Titus back to Corinth to help wrap things up before Paul arrives.

It is instructive to note what Paul calls this offering. He had just spoken of it as an act of Christian fellowship, a ministering to the saints (verse 4). Now he calls it an *act of grace*. He uses the same word that he does in verse one. It is a word he uses seven times, in fact, in these chapters. By doing so, he wants to tie everything connected with giving closely to the grace, the unmerited favor, the undeserved love, that God has given and continues to give to his people.

God's grace is a giving grace; it centers around his gift of Jesus Christ and his redemptive work on our behalf. That grace moves the Christian to be gracious — to freely, gladly give everything, including his material goods, back to the Lord. The offerings of Christians, then, are much more than bills and coins. They are a part of one's worship. The Christian who day by day is being "graced" by God acknowledges God's grace with freely-given, grace-motivated gifts.

In his intention to send Titus back to help the Corinthians finish gathering the offering, Paul is not implying that they will have to be coaxed or coerced to finish the work. Titus will be there simply to lend a helping hand. Paul is convinced that the spirituality of the Corinthians is such that they will welcome Titus into their midst to assist with the offering.

Paul is also confident that the Corinthians will be able to follow the example set by their Macedonian brothers and sisters. From what he knows of them personally and from what Titus has just reported to him, Paul can honestly say of the

Corinthians that they *excel,* literally "overflow," *in every-thing,* in every aspect of their new life in Christ — *in faith, in speech, in knowledge, in complete earnestness,* as well as in their love for Paul. Certainly they will also be able to *excel in the grace of giving.*

How positively, how evangelically Paul encourages their giving! He doesn't harangue them. He doesn't try to squeeze dead works out of their old Adam. He addresses the new man, who loves to go God's way and welcomes opportunities to express the gratitude of a reborn heart.

The Example of Jesus

8I am not commanding you, but I want to test the sincerity of your love by comparing it with the earnestness of others. 9For you know the grace of our Lord Jesus Christ, that though he was rich, yet for your sakes he became poor, so that you through his poverty might become rich.

The offerings a Christian brings are a fruit of faith, the response of a grateful heart to the goodness of God. That is why Paul is careful to say, *I am not commanding you.* He does not want this offering to be given reluctantly or grudgingly, as he will bring out in more detail in the next chapter.

He wants the Corinthians to be sure they understand why he has just held up the Macedonians as a model for them. It was not in an under-handed attempt to get more money out of them. He has not pointed them to an amount of money but to an attitude. He has reminded the Corinthians of the earnestness of their Macedonian sisters and brothers. He has spotlighted their zeal to give even though they had little themselves. He has demonstrated that they gave from a joyful heart. In all of this the Macedonians served as a fine example by which the Corinthians could measure the genuineness of their own love.

Then Paul turns to the example above all examples, that of Jesus. *You know the grace of our Lord Jesus Christ,* Paul tells them. This is something they already knew. He is not going to be telling them something they have not heard of before, but rather something they need to keep on hearing.

To describe the *grace of the Lord Jesus Christ,* Paul uses the same terms, *rich* and *poor,* he had been employing in talking about the offering. Here he applies these words to Jesus. *He was rich,* Paul reminds them. He is referring to the eternal riches that were his as the Son of God from all eternity. There was nothing that did not belong to him.

Yet *for your sakes,* Paul says, *he became poor.* He uses here the same word for "poor" that he had used to describe the Macedonians. It pictures an abject poverty, being reduced to the condition of a beggar. With these few words Paul is reminding the Corinthians of what Christians today refer to as Christ's state of humiliation. Writing to the Philippians, Paul put it this way: "He made himself nothing," literally, "emptied himself" (cf. Philippians 2:7).

The Macedonian Christians had very little; the very little they had they gave. Jesus had absolutely everything. He was Lord of the universe. And all of it he had given up. That he did, Paul tells the Corinthians, *so that you through his poverty might become rich.* "We are rich, for he was poor; is not this a wonder? Therefore, praise God evermore here on earth and yonder!" (TLH 97:3).

It is not difficult to see that the Jesus whom Paul holds up to the Corinthians as a perfect model of sacrificial giving is much more than a model. He is first of all a Savior. Through his humbling himself all the way to death, the Corinthians were now spiritually rich beyond compare. Their sins were forgiven. They were enjoying a brand new life as a part of the family of God. An eternity of joy awaited them.

They knew all of that, but they needed to remember it daily. If their eyes turned from the Christ who became poor that they might become rich, every area of their Christian life, including their stewardship practices, would soon degenerate into dead works instead of being good works. To be "grace gifts" their offerings must be grace-of-the-Lord-Jesus-Christ-driven gifts.

The Christ who became poor to make us rich is the foundation on which all Christian stewardship rests. He is Savior; he is Motivator; he is Example — and in that order. Saved by his grace, we are then motivated to follow his example, also in the area of giving.

An Appeal to Complete the Offering

10And here is my advice about what is best for you in this matter: Last year you were the first not only to give but also to have the desire to do so. 11Now finish the work, so that your eager willingness to do it may be matched by your completion of it, according to your means. 12For if the willingness is there, the gift is acceptable according to what one has, not according to what he does not have.

In the opening verses of this chapter Paul had offered various encouragements to the Corinthians to finish gathering in their offering for the poor in the church at Jerusalem. He had set the Macedonians before them as an example to emulate. He had pointed to the Corinthians' own spirituality, which was manifesting itself in many different ways. And, above all, he had turned their thoughts once more to the grace of the Lord Jesus Christ.

In the verses before us Paul offers what he hopes will be some practical, helpful advice to those whom he knows want to finish what they had begun. When the thought of gathering in such an offering had been broached about a year before the writing of 2 Corinthians, the Corinthian congregation had been the first to get involved. Theirs had been an eager involvement. Paul says that they were the first *to have the desire to do so.*

They had two things going for them: They had already begun to gather the offering, and they had a good attitude about it. They really wanted to be involved. Now they simply needed to *finish the work.* It was just a matter of their *eager willingness to do it* being *matched* by a *completion of it.*

Paul adds a significant phrase to this encouragement to get on with the work. Your giving, he says, should be *according to your means,* literally, "from what you have." That, one might think, should go without saying. How can one give from what one doesn't have? Isn't all giving from what one has?

Paul obviously has more in mind than that. He is talking about what we today often call proportionate giving, giving to the Lord in accordance with what he has given to us. The Corinthians should not be measuring their offerings by what others gave. They should not think that God is more pleased with the large offerings of others than he is with their relatively small offerings, as long as they are truly giving from what they have been given and are giving with a proper attitude.

Paul says just that when he tells the Corinthians, *If the willingness is there, the gift is acceptable according to what one has, not according to what he does not have.* If the heart is right, one does not have to worry about what he doesn't have. He doesn't have to be ashamed that he can give only a small offering. The poor widow gave from what she had, and Jesus praised her small, but large, offering (Mark 12:41-44). The larger offerings of the more wealthy are also pleasing to the Lord if they, with a willing heart, give from what they have. Think, for example, of the costly offering of love Mary poured on Jesus' feet. For that Jesus commended her (cf. John 12:1-8).

In the next verses Paul provides some helpful guidance for the Corinthian believers as they sought to determine how much they should give. He points out that they will want to keep two things in mind: The needs of those for whom this offering is being gathered as well as their own personal needs.

¹³Our desire is not that others might be relieved while you are hard pressed, but that there might be equality. ¹⁴At the present time your plenty will supply what they need, so that in turn their plenty will supply what you need. Then there will be equality,

The key word in these verses is *equality*. Paul docs not want the Corinthian believers to give so much that they themselves become *hard pressed,* in need of a relief offering themselves. On the other hand, they should recognize that at the present time they have more than they need while their sisters and brothers in Jerusalem have less than they need. *At the present time your plenty* (literally, "your surplus," that which was over and above what they needed for life), Paul says, *will supply what they need.* In that way there will be an equality.

Paul, we should note, is not advocating that all should put everything into one pot from which everyone could draw as he felt he had need. Rather, he is encouraging what he had earlier written to the Galatians, "As we have opportunity, let us do good to all people, especially to those who belong to the family of believers" (Galatians 6:10). The believers in

Jerusalem were the Corinthians' brothers and sisters. Giving from their *plenty,* from the extra God had given them, was a beautiful way for the believers in Corinth to express their fellowship, their oneness in Christ, with their poverty-stricken family members in Jerusalem.

In turn, Paul says, *their plenty will supply what you need. Then there will be equality.* It is difficult to say for sure what Paul means here. What kind of *plenty* did or would the Christians in Jerusalem have that could fill up something the Corinthians lacked? There are two possibilities. Paul could be referring to a time in the future when the tables might be turned. There could come a day when the Corinthians would suffer the kind of financial need the believers in Jerusalem were experiencing. Perhaps at that time the church in Jerusalem would be in a position to use its plenty to supply the Corinthians' need. That could be the kind of equality Paul is talking about: At times Christians may be on the giving end and at other times the receiving end of Christian charity.

A little more likely is the view that Paul is saying something similar to what he would write a few months later to the congregation at Rome: "If the Gentiles have shared in the Jews' spiritual blessings, they owe it to the Jews to share with them their material blessings" (Romans 15:27). In this interpretation Paul is saying to the Corinthians, "As you help the Jerusalem congregation physically with this offering, you will want to remember that they have helped and continue to help you spiritually since it is from Jerusalem, from the Jews, that God sent the Savior."

At any rate, Paul's point is that when Christians give from what God has given to them, they need never fear that they will be the poorer for doing so. God will always make things come out right. That is the implication of the Old Testament quotation with which Paul closes off this section:

¹⁵**as it is written: "He who gathered much did not have too much, and he who gathered little did not have too little."**

The quotation is from Exodus 16:18. It refers to the once-a-day gathering of manna in the wilderness. God's intention was that each one of the Israelites should have just enough to live on for the day. Some of the younger and stronger Israelites might have been able to gather much manna; some of the older and weaker ones might not have been able to pick up enough to last through the day. That would be no problem. Those with more than they needed would give to those with less than they needed. In that way each had enough.

Paul is saying that is the way it should be among the new Israel of God, the Church, each looking out not simply for his own needs but for the needs of others, whatever form those needs take. One person has much money; the other doesn't have enough to maintain his life. One person has been blessed with an abundance of the gospel of Jesus Christ; the other person doesn't know Christ or is just a spiritual infant. In both cases Christian love dictates that the first will use his plenty to help supply what the second lacks. In that way there is equality.

ASSISTANCE IN COMPLETING THE OFFERING: THE MISSION OF TITUS AND HIS COMPANIONS (8:16-9:5)

The practical issue that lay behind the stewardship instruction in 2 Corinthians 8 and 9 was the unfinished offering for the church in Jerusalem. In the opening verses of chapter eight, Paul spoke about the need to bring this offering to completion. It was important that the Corinthians "finish the work" (verse 11) they had begun. Paul also mentioned that when Titus came, probably bringing 2 Corinthians with him, he would help them with this work (cf. verse 6). Now he goes into more detail about the impending visit of Titus.

The Plan to Send Titus and the Brothers

16I thank God, who put into the heart of Titus the same concern I have for you. 17For Titus not only welcomed our appeal, but he is coming to you with much enthusiasm and on his own initiative.

Titus had the *same concern* for the believers in Corinth that Paul had. He shared with Paul the same Spirit-implanted, earnest desire that the Corinthians not only finish the offering but that they do so with the right kind of attitude.

That explains the response of Titus when Paul asked him to travel all the way back to Corinth, the place from which he had just come. Even though this meant a trip of about 200 miles, Titus not only accepted but *welcomed* Paul's appeal.

He was returning to Corinth not merely out of a sense of duty or of loyalty to Paul who had made this request of him. He was making this trip, says Paul, *with much enthusiasm and on his own initiative.*

The attitude Titus had toward helping with the completion of the offering was important. If he had consented to return to Corinth only with reluctance, this would have revealed itself in the way he went about his work. If this offering were to be a truly God-pleasing endeavor, not just those who gave it but those who helped to gather it needed to do so with a willing spirit.

Isn't that true today also? What a blessing it is when the members of a congregation's stewardship committee approach their work with enthusiasm. This they will do when they remember that their purpose is not simply to fund a budget. Rather, as Paul said earlier in this chapter, their mission is to help their fellow members "excel" in the "grace of giving" (verse 7).

In the verses that follow Paul tells the Corinthians that Titus would not be the only one traveling to Corinth to help with the offering.

18And we are sending along with him the brother who is praised by all the churches for his service to the gospel. 19What is more, he was chosen by the churches to accompany us as we carry the offering, which we administer in order to honor the Lord himself and to show our eagerness to help.

Paul was sending two people along with Titus (cf. verse 22). We aren't given the names of either of these two men; although, if they were from Macedonia, which seems fairly likely, we could probably narrow it down to four possibilities. Among the men who accompanied Paul to Jerusalem with the offering were three men from Macedonia: Sopater from Berea, and Aristarchus and Secundus from Thessalonica (cf. Acts 20:4). To that group we could add the name of Luke, who might have represented the congregation at Philippi in Macedonia, where he had evidently served during much of Paul's second and third missionary journeys.

Although we cannot be absolutely certain of the identity of these two men, we are given all the information about them we need. For one thing, Paul calls each of them a *brother,* that is, a fellow believer. Since gathering the funds to complete the offering for the poor at Jerusalem was a decidedly spiritual matter, it goes without saying that those whom Paul would use to help with this work would be fellow Christians.

Great care had been exercised in choosing these men. In speaking of the first of these two men, Paul mentions two factors which were taken into consideration. First, the man was *praised by all the churches for his service to the gospel.* When some years before this the Twelve had looked for people to help them with administering the affairs of the church in Jerusalem, they had sought men "known to be full of the Spirit and wisdom" (Acts 6:3). Spiritual work requires Spirit-filled workers. So it was with the work to be done in Corinth. Those entrusted with this ministry should be men with a good spiritual reputation. The "brother" Paul was sending with Titus met that criterion.

Secondly, Paul tells the Corinthians, this man was *chosen by the churches to accompany us as we carry the offering.* Once again, the word the NIV translates as "offering" is from the Greek word for "grace," a reminder that the offering is a "grace-gift," a freely given response to God's grace in Christ.

This offering, this gracious gift, was going to be brought to Jerusalem by Paul, together with representatives from the congregations involved in gathering it. Apparently the congregations themselves, not Paul, decided who would accompany Paul. The "brother" Paul was sending to Corinth along with Titus was one of those congregationally-chosen representatives. This served as further evidence that the Corinthians could receive him with full confidence.

Paul explains why he was taking such care with every aspect of this offering, including the choice of people who would help gather it. He mentions two things. First, he says, he was administering the offering *to honor the Lord himself.* More than money was involved here. This offering was a way of worshiping God. King Solomon had put it this way in the book of Proverbs: "Honor the Lord with your wealth, with the firstfruits of all your crops" (Proverbs 3:9). Paul, conscious of this truth, was taking pains that every aspect of the offering, both the giving and the gathering, would be carried out in a way that gave glory to God.That was one thing Paul was constantly aware of: The offering was to give praise and glory to God.

Secondly, Paul says that he and the "brothers" are involved in this offering *to show our eagerness to help.* What Paul means here is not entirely clear. The NIV translation adds the words *to help,* which are not in the original text, as a way of explaining this phrase. But that still leaves the question, "Help whom?"

The best commentary on the phrase is perhaps to be found in verses 11 and 12 of this same chapter. In these verses Paul uses the same Greek word that the NIV translates here with *eagerness.* In verses 11 and 12 it translates the word with "eager willingness" and "willingness." There Paul was talking about the Corinthians' attitude toward the offering, their "eager willingness" to take part in it.

In the verse before us, it appears that Paul, by using the same word, is saying that just as the Corinthians have demonstrated an eagerness to give, so he is eager to do everything possible to help them bring this offering to a God-honoring completion.

A right attitude is of primary importance on the part of those who give the offering and of those who gather it. Paul and the brothers he is sending demonstrate such a spirit.

Paul explains further why he has been so careful in his handling of this offering:

20We want to avoid any criticism of the way we administer this liberal gift.

The word translated *liberal gift* in this verse is found only here in the Bible. It comes from a word which means "thick" or "bulky," and then "abundant." A translation that brings out this thought more fully might be "large sum." By the time the whole offering was gathered together and ready to be taken to Jerusalem, it would add up to a significant amount. Paul knew this, and accordingly he wanted to be extremely careful in how he handled it.

As has been made clear repeatedly in this letter, Paul was well aware that there were some in Corinth who opposed him. They had even used the seemingly minor matter of his change of travel plans to label him as untrustworthy. And Paul also knew that criticism of him personally could affect the way people responded to his gospel ministry. He therefore was making every effort to *avoid any criticism* of the way he was gathering this large offering and bringing it to Jerusalem.

It probably would have been easier for Paul to have done this work alone than to coordinate the work of several men. As it turned out, at least eight men, the seven mentioned in Acts 20:4 and Luke, accompanied Paul to Jerusalem with the offering. This had a positive benefit, of course. The coming of these men from Macedonia, Achaia, Asia, and Galatia would visibly demonstrate the close bond of fellowship that existed between the churches Paul had founded and the mother church in Jerusalem.

It was, however, also a preventive measure on the part of Paul. His enemies would not be able to accuse him of shady dealing, of putting some of the offering into his own pocket. Not only was Paul going to bring along eight witnesses, but eight witnesses with impeccable reputations, men chosen by their own congregations to accompany Paul.

The men he was bringing with him represented the givers of the offering: the churches of Galatia, Asia, Macedonia, and Achaia. This would protect Paul from another charge his detractors might hurl at him: that by this offering he was trying to glorify himself as the great benefactor of the Jerusalem church. The presence of these representatives of the churches would make it clear that the offering was much more than a one-man show.

21For we are taking pains to do what is right, not only in the eyes of the Lord but also in the eyes of men.

With these words Paul makes it clear that in this situation it was not enough for him to be able to say, "God knows that I am handling this offering in an honorable way," and then to carry it out in a way that might have aroused the suspicions of others. He knew that he needed to concern himself not only with what he was doing but with people's perceptions of what he was doing. In a previous chapter Paul had said, "We put no stumbling block in anyone's path, so that our ministry will not be discredited" (6:3). That was the way in which he was handling every aspect of the offering.

Isn't this sound advice even today? Writing to Timothy, Paul says that leaders in the church must be "above reproach" (1 Timothy 3:2). That certainly applies to the way a congregation's offerings are handled. There should not be even a hint of impropriety, certainly not before God, but also not before people.

Paul now gives us a brief glimpse at the other "brother" he is sending to Corinth:

22In addition, we are sending with them our brother who has often proved to us in many ways that he is zealous, and now even more so because of his great confidence in you.

This *brother,* too, is not named, but Paul does tell us two things about him that qualify him for this significant task. For one thing, says Paul, he *has often proved to us in many ways that he is zealous.* The word translated *proved* comes from a Greek word that has in it the idea of "tested." But more than that, it implies a successful passing of the test. The adjectival form of the word was used to describe coins that had passed the test, coins which were "genuine," not counterfeit.

The *brother* Paul was sending to Corinth along with Titus and the other brother was not a novice. He was a mature Christian who had already been tested in other areas of service. He had passed these tests. There was no doubt in Paul's mind that this man was *zealous* with a zeal that was tried and tested. Paul was convinced that his was not the kind of zeal that would burn brightly at first but then in the face of difficulty would sputter and go out. Paul knew that this brother was both eager and able to serve effectively throughout this vital undertaking.

This serves as a good reminder to Christian congregations today to choose with care those who will lead them in their stewardship endeavors. It is not the place to put a new Christian or, for that matter, one who has been a Christian for some time but has not been tested and found to be *zealous* for carrying out the Lord's work in the Lord's way.

The second thing Paul tells us about this brother is that he had *great confidence* in the Corinthians. We are not told how he had gained such confidence in them. The most likely possibility is that he, too, had heard the report of Titus upon his return from Corinth (cf. 7:6-15).

At any rate, his confidence in his fellow believers in Corinth would make him a good addition to the team being sent to Corinth. He would be expecting, not the worst, but the best from the Corinthians.

There is a lesson here for Christian leaders of all times. Whether it is in the area of stewardship or any other aspect of the believer's life of sanctification, it is important to remember that Christians according to the new man love to do the Lord's will. They can, therefore, be approached with confidence that they will respond favorably to guidance from the word, also in the matter of God-pleasing ways to use their material possessions. To expect the worst out of God's people is not scriptural. It also tends to be a self-fulfilling prophecy.

In the two verses that follow Paul urges the Corinthians to welcome warmly the delegation he is sending to them.

23As for Titus, he is my partner and fellow worker among you; as for our brothers, they are representatives of the churches and an honor to Christ. 24Therefore show these men the proof of your love and the reason for our pride in you, so that the churches can see it.

This is the ministry team Paul is dispatching to Corinth: Titus and the two *brothers.* Titus would evidently be serving as the leader of this group. The Corinthians already knew and respected him, Paul says, as a *fellow worker among you,* or, as it might be translated, "fellow worker in your service." Paul, therefore, doesn't have to say much by way of a note of recommendation. He simply reminds them that Titus was his *partner;* when the Corinthians received him, they were in effect also receiving Paul.

The two *brothers* evidently were not personally known by the Corinthians; otherwise Paul would certainly have mentioned them by name. That is why he spent a little more time introducing them. He summarizes what he has said about them by calling them *representatives of the churches and an honor to Christ.* The word translated "representatives" is literally "apostles," which means "those who are sent out." The New Testament uses this word in more than one way. More often than not it refers to the Twelve plus Paul, those specially chosen and commissioned representatives of Christ.

But at times the word is used a little more broadly, as here, for example, where it refers to those who have been commissioned by their churches to carry out a certain mission. The mission here was to represent their churches in gathering the offering and bringing it to Jerusalem.

Secondly, Paul says these men are *an honor to Christ,* literally, "the glory of Christ." Their Christian character was such that it reflected something of the brightness of Christ's beauty and glory. Certainly, the believers in Corinth would not have to hesitate to receive these men. They were not like those he had warned about previously in this letter, the ones who "peddle the word of God for profit" (2:17).

That is why Paul could without hesitation urge the Corinthians to open their hearts to these men. He tells them, *Show these men the proof of your love.* Earlier in this letter Paul had pleaded that the Corinthians not withhold their affection from him (cf. 6:11-13). Now he exhorts them to demonstrate visibly their love for these brothers who were coming to help them.

It appears that Paul had already assured this delegation that it would be warmly received, for he says to the Corinthians, *Show these men . . . the reason for our pride in you.* Let them, and in that way also the churches they represent, see that Paul wasn't wrong when he spoke in glowing terms about the congregation in Corinth.

Having introduced the delegation which would be arriving with this letter, Paul now goes on to emphasize the importance of finishing the offering.

The Urgency of Completing the Offering

9 **There is no need for me to write to you about this service to the saints. [2]For I know your eagerness to help, and I have been boasting about it to the Macedonians, telling them that since last year you in Achaia were ready to give; and your enthusiasm has stirred most of them to action.**

There is a careful balance between these verses and the three that follow. In the Greek this is demonstrated by the use of words which could be translated "on the one hand . . . but on the other hand . . ." In speaking this way Paul was exercising excellent tact.

On the one hand, it was true that the Corinthians really didn't have to hear anything more about this *service to the saints* in Jerusalem. Paul already knew about their *eagerness to help.* He uses here the same word he had used in 8:11, 12, and 19. The Corinthians had already demonstrated a readiness, an eager willingness, to participate in the offering.

In fact, says Paul, *I have been boasting about it* (literally, "about you") *to the Macedonians.* With these words Paul wasn't patting himself on the back. He had not been boasting about what he had managed to get the Corinthians to do, but rather about what the Lord had moved them to do in response to the "grace of the Lord Jesus Christ" (8:9).

This, says Paul, is what I boasted about to the Macedonians: *Since last year you in Achaia were ready to give.* Achaia was the province of which Corinth was the capital. Two other cities in Achaia are mentioned in the New Testament: Cenchrea, one of Corinth's ports in which there was a Christian congregation (cf. Romans 16:1), and Athens, where there were at least some believers, if not a congregation as such (cf. Acts 17:33).

Even before the writing of 1 Corinthians, in which Paul had provided some guidance for the mechanics of the offering (cf. 1 Corinthians 16:1-4), the congregations in Achaia had clearly indicated their readiness to participate in it. And they were still willing to be involved. Paul uses a form of the Greek verb which indicates that what was true in the past was still in effect. The Christians in Achaia had been and still were *ready to give.*

Your enthusiasm, Paul tells them, *has stirred most of them,* that is, the Macedonian Christians, *to action.* With the words *most of them* Paul was being a realist. The sanctification level of some of the Macedonians was such that the example of the Corinthians didn't affect them. But the vast majority of the believers in Macedonia were encouraged and stimulated to action by the example the Corinthians had set.

It is interesting to see how Paul could hold up the Macedonians as an example for the Corinthians to follow (cf. 8:1-8) while at the same time he used the Corinthians as a model for the Macedonians to emulate. The Corinthians had served as an example to the Macedonians by their eagerness to undertake this offering; now the Macedonians could serve as an example to the Corinthians by the way they had followed through with the offering.

Christians today will not want to overlook the value of both being an example and of learning from the example of others. In this way Christians can "spur one another on toward love and good deeds" (Hebrews 10:24).

That is the one side of Paul's "on the one hand . . . but on the other hand . . ." approach in the first five verses of this chapter. Wisely, with Christian love and tact, he begins with the positive statement that he doesn't really have to say anything more about this offering to them. That's "the one hand." Then comes "the other hand."

3But I am sending the brothers in order that our boasting about you in this matter should not prove hollow, but that you may be ready, as I said you would be.

Paul was a realist. He knew that what people plan and purpose does not always materialize. He was well acquainted with the turmoil the church in Corinth had been going through during the past year. He had written 1 Corinthians in response to the many problems in the church. A church in turmoil might easily put on the back burner such an endeavor as an offering for believers in a far-off place. A gentle reminder, then, that the Corinthians think about finishing what they had begun was very much in place.

Paul had been boasting about the preparedness of the Corinthians. He didn't want that boasting to turn out to be *hollow,* empty words. That is why he was *sending the brothers,* the three men mentioned in 8:16-24, to them. They would help the believers there to complete the offering they had already indicated they were very much ready to participate in. The Corinthians, therefore, should not resent the visit of this delegation, but welcome it.

"Let us encourage one another," writes the author of Hebrews (Hebrews 10:25). Christians will certainly not just grudgingly tolerate but gladly receive the encouragement of their fellow believers — also in the area of stewardship of their material goods.

Paul explains further why he was sending this advance delegation to Corinth:

⁴For if any Macedonians come with me and find you unprepared, we — not to say anything about you — would be ashamed of having been so confident.

Paul isn't talking here about the two men he was sending along with Titus, but rather about other members of the churches in Macedonia who might accompany Paul to Corinth. Paul had been telling them how eagerly the Corinthians had accepted the idea of gathering an offering to help the poor believers in Jerusalem. How embarrassing it would be for them to arrive in Corinth and find that the Corinthians' good intentions had not resulted in appropriate action.

Embarrassing to whom? Both to Paul and to the Corinthians: *We — not to say anything about you — would be ashamed of having been so confident.* The confidence Paul is speaking about here was his conviction that the Corinthians would finish the work they had begun. If they did not finish it, he would be ashamed that he had been so vocally confident about this matter.

See how evangelically Paul deals with the situation. The Corinthians, too, would be ashamed if they quit before finishing. Paul does not want to emphasize that, however, lest he lead them to complete the offering for the wrong reason. They should not finish the work because they would be mortified if they didn't. They should finish this grace-gift as a faith response to "the grace of the Lord Jesus Christ" (8:9). Yet, out of love for the Corinthians, Paul feels constrained to mention what might happen if the Macedonians came with him and found them *unprepared*. He doesn't want them to suffer any embarrassment.

⁵So I thought it necessary to urge the brothers to visit you in advance and finish the arrangements for the generous gift you had promised. Then it will be ready as a generous gift, not as one grudgingly given.

By the *brothers* Paul means Titus and his two companions (8:16-24) who would be Paul's advance men. The Greek of this verse brings this out even more clearly. Three words in the first sentence have a prefix which means "beforehand" or "in advance." The three-man delegation from Paul was to come to Corinth in advance to complete arrangements in advance for the offering the Corinthians had promised in advance. The result? By the time Paul and possibly some of the Macedonians arrived in Corinth everything would be done.

Paul calls the offering a *generous gift*. This is another in a series of decidedly spiritual terms Paul uses to depict this offering. In 8:4 and 9:1 he had described it as an act of service, or ministry, as the word can also be translated. The offering was "service [or 'ministry'] to the saints." It wasn't simply moving money from one place to another. As the Corinthians and others in the churches Paul had founded served the needs of their fellow believers in Jerusalem, they were engaging in acts of Christian ministry.

In 8:6, 7, and 19 Paul had used the Greek word for "grace" to characterize the offering. It was a "grace-gift." This emphasizes a key attitude that lies behind a believer's offerings: They are a response to the grace, the undeserved love, of Christ who became poor that we might become rich. Christ has freely given to us; now in gratitude for his grace we will freely give.

In the verse before us we see another name Paul gives to this offering. The word appears twice. The NIV translates it both times with the words *generous gift*. The word literally means "blessing." With this term Paul is apparently describing the offering in terms of what it will be for the recipients, the believers in Jerusalem. For them the offering will be not merely a bag of gold and silver coins but a blessing of God brought into their lives through the hands of their believing sisters and brothers in the Gentile world.

The Christians in Achaia and all the other places Paul had worked had been on the receiving end of God's bountiful blessings. He had given them what they needed — for their souls and also for their bodies. Now, with the extra material wealth with which God had blessed them, they could be a blessing to others. The blessed would become blessers.

To help make sure that the offering be just that, that it come from a heart which gratefully recognizes God's blessings and, therefore, wants to bless others in return, Paul *thought it necessary* to send the advance delegation to Corinth. It was important that the offering truly be a *generous gift*, a blessing from the blessed, *not as one grudgingly given*, or, to put it more literally, "not as covetousness."

There are two different opinions as to what Paul means with the words "not as covetousness." Some think Paul is contrasting a willing gift on the part of the Corinthians with a gift that Paul greedily pressures them to give. The covetousness then would be on the part of Paul, who wants their money. Paul was charged with just that by his opponents, as is brought out in 2 Corinthians 12 (verses 14-18). Obviously, he doesn't want anyone to reach such a conclusion about the offering.

It seems, however, that the way the NIV interprets these words is more in keeping with the immediate context. It is best to see the Corinthians as being portrayed in both phrases. Paul's prayer is that this offering will come out of willing and generous hearts rather than covetous hearts which part with material goods only reluctantly and grudgingly.

Once again we see that Paul's primary concern is the attitude of the heart. Offerings that proceed from a heart that has been warmed by the grace and blessings of God will be expressions of praise and thanks to God. Such offerings, whether the amount is large or small, will be acceptable to him and a true blessing to the recipient.

BLESSED RESULTS OF THE OFFERING
(9:6-15)

Paul wrote 2 Corinthians 8 and 9 in direct response to a specific situation in the congregation at Corinth: The offering to provide assistance to the poverty-stricken believers in Jerusalem had begun well but then had started to flounder.

He wrote these chapters both to encourage the Corinthians to finish the offering (8:1-15) and to offer them assistance in bringing it to completion (8:16-9:5). To encourage them, Paul pointed to the example of the Macedonian believers as well as to the past performance of the Corinthians themselves. Above all, he directed their thoughts to Jesus, who became poor so they could become rich with the gifts of forgiveness, new spiritual life, and the assurance of an eternal salvation.

To help the Corinthians complete the offering, Paul was sending Titus and two others to Corinth. The closing verses of chapter 8 served as a letter of recommendation from Paul for these men. Paul was not sending them because the Corinthians were incapable of finishing or unwilling to finish the work on their own. Time was of the essence at this point, however, since Paul was on the verge of leaving for Jerusalem. Paul could see that the Corinthians would benefit from some brother to brother encouragement and assistance in completing this work. His prayer was that the Corinthians would receive these men in the spirit in which they had been sent. They were not coming to coerce them to give but to help them bring to completion an offering the Corinthians wanted to give.

Now, in the final verses of these two chapters, Paul talks about some blessings that will result from this offering.

The Giver Is Blessed

⁶Remember this: Whoever sows sparingly will also reap sparingly, and whoever sows generously will also reap generously.

Paul uses an illustration here that would have been quite familiar to his hearers. He pictures two farmers sowing seed in their fields. The one sows his seed *sparingly*. He is stingy in the amount of seed he puts into the ground, hoping in this way to save a little money. Such action is short-sighted, however. In the end the farmer will be the poorer, for sparse sowing results in a sparse, meager harvest.

The second farmer approaches his work in an entirely different manner. He sows his seed *generously*. The word translated *generously* is the same one we find in verse 5, where the NIV translated it as "generous gift." As was brought out in the discussion of that verse, the word literally means "blessing." The offering, Paul said, will be a "blessing" to the church in Jerusalem.

The same idea is found here, only this time the blessing is described as coming back to the one who sows the seed. The picture is that of a farmer sowing seed in anticipation of being blessed by that sowing. He knows that what he puts into the ground will come back to him many times over. It would be foolish, therefore, to be miserly in his sowing. The way to be assured of the blessing of a generous, bountiful harvest is to be generous in one's sowing.

Paul applies the truth of this proverbial saying to the subject of giving and in so doing echoes the thought of several of the Proverbs. "One man gives freely, yet gains even more;

another withholds unduly, but comes to poverty" (11:24). "A generous man will himself be blessed" (22:9). "Honor the Lord with your wealth, with the firstfruits of all your crops; then your barns will be filled to overflowing, and your vats will brim over with new wine" (3:9,10).

The Lord spoke in a similar way in the book of the prophet Malachi: " 'Bring the whole tithe into the storehouse. . . . Test me in this,' says the Lord Almighty, 'and see if I will not throw open the floodgates of heaven and pour out so much blessing that you will not have room enough for it' " (Malachi 3:10).

Paul is saying the same thing here. Just as a sower knows that the seed he has sown is not wasted but will result in a harvest, so those who give an offering for the Jerusalem believers should be sure that their offering will not be without effect. The obvious benefactors will be the poor in Jerusalem, the place where the seed of the offering will be sown. Paul's point here, however, is that blessings will also come back upon those who sowed the seed of the offering. Generous sowing, a generous offering, will result in a generous harvest for them. They can sow with confidence in anticipation of this blessing.

When we look at the verses which follow, we will see some examples of the kind of generous harvest Paul has in mind. We should note at this point, however, that we are not understanding Paul properly if we reduce what he says here to a simplistic, "The more money you Corinthians give, the more money you will get." That is pressing the comparison of sowing and harvesting beyond Paul's intention. What he wants the Corinthians to be sure of is that God's bountiful blessings, which come in various forms, will always attend their giving.

The same holds true today. As God's children give, and give generously, they can do so in anticipation that God blesses Christian giving. As he blesses the generous sower, he blesses the generous giver.

7Each man should give what he has decided in his heart to give, not reluctantly or under compulsion, for God loves a cheerful giver.

This verse underscores a key difference between believers living under the old covenant and those living under the new covenant. In the Malachi passage quoted above the word "tithe" is mentioned. Believers under the old covenant lived under the law of the tithe. If they had asked, "How much should I give?", the answer would have been, "God says that you must give back to him one-tenth of what he gives to you."

Believers living under the new covenant are no longer under law but under grace. The Corinthians were living under the new covenant. If they, therefore, were to ask Paul, "How much do you expect us to give?", his response would have been what he writes in this verse, "It is a matter of each one giving *what he has decided in his heart to give.*" They were free to choose for themselves what amount to give.

With freedom comes responsibility. So it is in the matter of giving under the new covenant. If the Corinthians were free to choose for themselves what to give, that implied two things. For one thing, they could not ignore the responsibility which that freedom gave them. They were responsible for planning their giving. Secondly, they needed to be aware that this planning process would be aided by the new man living in them, but it would also be obstructed by the old man. The Corinthians had the responsibility of making sure that they knew who was talking and of listening to the right voice.

One way of identifying these competing voices, as Christians plan their giving, is to remember that the old man gives only *reluctantly or under compulsion.* The word translated *reluctantly* literally means "out of grief." The old man is marked by covetousness. It grieves him to part with money unless it is being used for a selfish end.

The old man will give to help others only *under compulsion.* Our Lutheran Confessions, in Article IV of the *Formula of Concord,* quote this phrase. They speak of giving *under compulsion* as an action "which is wrung from one against his will, by force or otherwise, so that he acts externally for appearance, but, nevertheless, without and against his will."

The new man, on the other hand, is *a cheerful giver.* The word translated *cheerful* is found only one other time in the Bible. Paul in Romans speaks of a person with the spiritual gift of "showing mercy." If one has that gift, says Paul, then "let him do it cheerfully" (Romans 12:8).

From this word we get the English word "hilarious." The new man finds great joy and happiness in using every gift God has given for the benefit of others. The new man remembers that God himself is a cheerful giver. He didn't even spare his own Son. Such cheerful giving on the part of God inspires the Christian to be a cheerful giver.

When Christians are deciding in their hearts what to give, how can they be sure they will listen to the right voice, the voice that promotes cheerful, generous, as-God-has-given-to-me giving? Luther's answer in the *Small Catechism* still stands. He urges us to go back daily to our baptism and claim its blessings anew. We do that when by "daily contrition and repentance" we drown our Old Adam "with its evil deeds and desires," and with that let the new man "day by day . . . arise, as from the dead, to live in the presence of

God in righteousness and purity." As the old man is put to death, the new man is given the opportunity to live and flourish and guide the Christian's life, also when he decides in his heart what to give.

8And God is able to make all grace abound to you, so that in all things at all times, having all that you need, you will abound in every good work.

Note how often Paul uses the words "all" or "every" to emphasize why the Corinthians don't have to hesitate to be generous, cheerful givers. The God of *all* grace will see to it that in *all* things and at *all* times the Corinthians will have *all* they need so they can abound in *every* good work.

With these words Paul is assuring the Corinthians that they will be able to put into practice the kind of cheerful, generous giving he has been talking about. They will be able to do this because God himself will be at work in their lives, God who *is able to make all grace abound to them.* All the riches of God's marvelous grace, a grace that moved him to send his Son, a grace that through the gospel had brought forgiveness and faith to the Corinthians — that grace would move them to be cheerful givers.

God's grace in all its rich variety would continue to *abound,* literally, "overflow," in the lives of the Corinthians. It would make them certain that the God who had given them Jesus would also give them all they needed so that they could *abound in every good work.* God's abounding grace would result in abounding good works, among which would be the good work of cheerful and generous giving.

Paul then uses a verse from one of the Psalms to back up this contention.

⁹As it is written:

> **"He has scattered abroad his gifts to the poor;**
> **his righteousness endures forever."**

The verse is taken from Psalm 112 (verse 9), which is paired very closely with the 111th Psalm. Psalm 111 emphasizes the generosity of God in showering his blessings upon his people. This parallels Paul's words about God being able to *make all grace abound.* Psalm 112 describes the response of the believer to the generosity of God. He will generously share God's gifts with others. He will, as Paul has just put it, *abound in every good work.*

The verse Paul quotes here, taken from Psalm 112, is not talking about what God does, as one might suppose when he first reads it. Rather, the verse is describing what a believing child of God does in response to God's generosity. In his new life of righteousness, which is the gift of a gracious God, the believer does as God has done for him: *he scatters abroad his gifts to the poor.* He gives to others as God has given and continues to give to him.

¹⁰Now he who supplies seed to the sower and bread for food will also supply and increase your store of seed and will enlarge the harvest of your righteousness. ¹¹You will be made rich in every way so that you can be generous on every occasion, and through us your generosity will result in thanksgiving to God.

With these words Paul returns to the seed-sowing imagery of verse 6. He explains how the grateful believer will be able to do what the Psalm 112 quotation says he will do. The farmer can depend on God, not just to produce a harvest, but to give him the seeds for sowing through which God produces the harvest.

So it is with the believer. God not only promises bountiful blessings to the cheerful, generous giver, but he supplies him with what he needs so he is able to give. Paul assures the Corinthian believers that the same God who makes sure the farmer has seed for sowing *will also supply and increase their store of seed,* that is, the money and other material goods they need to be able to give.

And he will also, says Paul, *enlarge your harvest of righteousness.* Paul here picks up on the phrase, *His* [the believer's] *righteousness endures forever,* from the Psalm passage he had just quoted. With the word *righteousness* he is broadening the picture somewhat. He wants to make it clear that when he talks about Christian giving, he is talking about an aspect of the Christian's life of sanctification. A person who has been declared righteous by faith in Jesus is now able to live a righteous, godly life. The harvest, or fruit, of being declared not guilty, or righteous, by faith in Jesus is the believer's life of righteousness. One aspect of this new, godly life is a godly attitude toward giving.

With these words Paul is not only assuring believing children of God that God will always give us what we need so we can give generously. With the promise that God *will enlarge the harvest of your righteousness* Paul is also assuring us that God will continue to strengthen us in our lives of sanctification so that we have an attitude that produces neither reluctant nor coerced, but rather cheerful, giving.

Paul repeats this thought with the words, *You will be made rich in every way.* Note the word *every.* The Corinthians would not simply be given sufficient "seed," that is, money, so they could participate in the offering. They would also *be made rich* in a spiritual way. The Lord would continue to strengthen the new man in them so their giving would be from a proper attitude of the heart.

That is underscored by the word the NIV translates here as *generous*. Paul had already used the word in chapter 8, verse 2. It means "single-mindedness" and thus speaks not so much of amount as it does of attitude. In this context it has the idea of giving that comes from a sincere heart, giving that has no ulterior motives. Believers who are being *made rich in every way,* in whose hearts the Spirit is working daily to produce the harvest of a righteous life, will be able to give in this *generous,* single-minded way *on every occasion.*

The result of this kind of single-minded, sincere giving, Paul writes, will be that *through us your generosity will result in thanksgiving to God.* By us Paul likely means himself and his companions who will carry the offering to Jerusalem. When the offering is received, the believers in Jerusalem will be thankful. Their thanks, however, will extend not only to those who gave the gift but also especially to their gracious God who had instilled such a single-minded, sincere heart of love in their brothers and sisters.

The Corinthians truly could anticipate God's blessings as they gave. So can Christians today. He will provide us with the means to give. We give from what he gives to us, as the hymn-writer puts it, "We give Thee but Thine own, whate'er the gift may be," (TLH 441). And through the gospel, the good news of what he has done for us through Jesus, the Holy Spirit will continue to instill in us the desire to give.

God Is Glorified

[12]**This service that you perform is not only supplying the needs of God's people but is also overflowing in many expressions of thanks to God.**

With the words the NIV translates as *this service that you perform* Paul makes it clear that the offering had a vertical as

167

well as a horizontal aspect to it. The giving of this offering was a part of their worship of God. Paul uses a word from which we get our English word "liturgy." The ancient Greeks used it to describe some public service an individual performed for his country, usually without remuneration. In the Bible it has to do with service that a Christian performs for his Lord. It was used, for example, of Zechariah, the father of John the Baptist, to describe his work as a priest in the temple (cf. Luke 1:23). When Christians give offerings, they are serving their Lord no less than the priests who offered up sacrifices to the Lord. We worship God with our offerings.

In these verses Paul points to another way God is worshiped and glorified through a Christian's offerings. It is something he had already referred to at the end of verse 11. Those on the receiving end of the Corinthians' offerings, the believers in Jerusalem, whose lack was being supplied by these gifts, would also be moved to worship and glorify God. Not only the giver, therefore, but also the receiver would worship and praise God in connection with this same offering.

This thanksgiving to God, in fact, was already occurring even before the offering had arrived. Paul uses a present tense verb here. Your *service,* Paul says, besides supplying the needs of God's people, *is also overflowing in many expressions of thanks to God.* Just knowing of the concern of their sisters and brothers in Christ filled the Jerusalem saints with an overwhelming desire to thank the Lord.

In 1 Corinthians Paul had urged that whatever the Corinthians did they should do "for the glory of God" (1 Corinthians 10:31). That certainly applies to the subject of giving, whether it be on the part of the giver or the recipient. The giver gives out of thankfulness to God; the receiver receives with thankfulness to God.

¹³**Because of the service by which you have proved yourselves, men will praise God for the obedience that accompanies your confession of the gospel of Christ, and for your generosity in sharing with them and with everyone else.**

With this verse Paul becomes a little more specific. He explains what it was especially about this offering that was causing the believers in Jerusalem to be overflowing with thanksgiving to God. He tells the Corinthians, "Your brothers and sisters in Jerusalem are praising God *because of the service by which you have proved yourselves.*" With the words translated *proved yourselves* Paul uses a word he had already used in 8:2. It has the idea of having successfully passed a test. It was used, as mentioned previously, to describe coins that were genuine, not counterfeit.

So it was with this offering. This offering of love provided concrete evidence to the Christians at Jerusalem that the Gentile converts in such far-away places as Corinth or Philippi or Ephesus were genuine believers.

A genuine confession of faith will produce fruits that are in keeping with that confession. There will be, as Paul puts it, an *obedience,* a submission to God's will, *that accompanies* one's *confession of the gospel of Christ.* That is what the Christians in Jerusalem could see in this offering. The Gentile converts in the various places Paul had worked were clearly practicing what they professed.

Paul further explains that the Jerusalem believers were praising God for the Corinthians' *generosity in sharing with them and with everyone else.* The word translated generosity is the third occurrence in chapters 8 and 9 of the word that is more literally translated "single-mindedness" (cf. 8:2 and 9:11).

Again, by using this word, Paul is not so much talking about the amount of money as he is talking about the sincere attitude of love and concern they have for their fellow believers. Though the churches at Corinth and Jerusalem were separated by many miles of land and water, they were held together in a close bond of Christian fellowship. The Corinthians were expressing that fellowship by the offering of love that was in the process of being gathered and then would be brought to Jerusalem.

Paul continues with this thought in the verse that follows.

Bonds of Christian Fellowship Are Strengthened

14And in their prayers for you their hearts will go out to you, because of the surpassing grace God has given you.

This is a continuation of Paul's thought at the close of verse 13, where he mentioned yet another blessing that God was attaching to this offering. Not only would the Corinthians be able to help alleviate a critical physical need through the offering. Not only would this offering be a way by which the Corinthians could worship their God from whom all blessings flow. Not only would the offering result in thanksgiving to God on the part of those who received it. The offering would also strengthen the ties of Christian fellowship between the church in Jerusalem, which consisted largely of Jews, and the churches Paul had founded, which were made up primarily of Gentiles.

To fully appreciate what this means, one has to remember the attitude Jews had toward Gentiles. They wanted to have nothing to do with them. It had even been difficult to convince the Jewish Christians that the gospel, without any restrictions, was meant also for the Gentile world.

Peter, for example, had to be taught by a direct vision from God not to "call anything impure that God has made clean" (Acts 10:15). Even after that Peter had not been entirely consistent in his approach to the Gentiles. On one occasion, while in Antioch of Syria, he had made the Gentile Christians feel as though they were second-class Christians when he stopped fraternizing with them upon the arrival of some Jewish Christians from Jerusalem (cf. Galatians 2:11-13).

Now, says Paul, the hearts of the Jewish believers in Jerusalem were going out to their Gentile brothers and sisters in the faith in Corinth. Quite a remarkable change!

Note what produced this change. It wasn't simply the money that was coming their way from Corinth. Rather, it was what that money represented. In this offering the Jewish Christians saw evidence of the *surpassing grace* God had given to the Gentiles. The offering made it clear that the gospel had been just as effective among the Gentiles as among the Jews. This outpouring of love across the seas from Corinth to Jerusalem demonstrated that the Holy Spirit had done the same work in the hearts of the Gentiles as he had in the hearts of the Jewish believers. It was a beautiful expression of Christian fellowship that bound them together into one body, even though they were separated by many miles.

A similar scenario is repeated time and again even today. When we as Christians in the United States bring offerings to support other Christians in mission fields around the world, it is a way by which we express our fellowship in Christ with them. And they recognize that. More often than we might think, the hearts of our fellow Christians in Central Africa or Southeast Asia or South America go out to their brothers and sisters in the United States. They thank God for the surpassing grace he has given to them, which has moved them to be so generous with their offerings.

Offerings for missions are not simply money flowing from here to there. They are love, Christian love, in action. They are expressions of Christian fellowship extending from one continent to another, helping to bind even more closely together those whom the Spirit through the gospel has already made one.

¹⁵Thanks be to God for his indescribable gift!

These are fitting words with which to close this entire section. The *indescribable gift* Paul is speaking of here is God's grace (cf. verse 14). Throughout 2 Corinthians 8 and 9 Paul has kept our thoughts focused on God's grace. He has reminded us of the grace of God's Son: "You know the grace of our Lord Jesus Christ, that though he was rich, yet for your sakes he became poor, so that you through his poverty might become rich" (8:9). Through the grace of Jesus we enjoy the riches of forgiveness, new life, and the promise of eternal life. That grace in turn moves and empowers Christians to bring their grace-gifts, their offerings, in thankful response to God's grace.

In these two chapters Paul has pointed to a number of things Christians are doing as they bring their offerings. With their offerings Christians are:

- Worshiping God
- Helping to alleviate the spiritual and physical needs of others
- Inspiring others to thank and praise God
- Serving as an example for other Christians to emulate
- Expressing their Christian fellowship with the brothers and sisters in Christ who benefit from their offerings.

Christians, therefore, moved and empowered by the grace of God in Christ, will, as Paul has brought out in these chapters:

- Look upon giving as a privilege, not a chore
- Give cheerfully, not reluctantly or under compulsion
- Give proportionately, from what God has given to them
- Trust God to supply what they need
- Value the example others set and seek to be positive examples themselves
- Welcome the guidance and encouragement of their Christian brothers and sisters in the matter of giving, just as they do in every other aspect of their life of sanctification
- Rejoice to work together with their fellow Christians in using their offerings jointly for God's glory and the advancement of his Kingdom.

The grace of Jesus. The grace of giving. These two are closely tied together. The first will inevitably result in the second. For both, says Paul, *thanks be to God*.

As a postscript to chapters 8 and 9, we might want to inquire if the Corinthians did actually finish gathering in the offering. From his letter to the Romans, written about two months after the writing of 2 Corinthians, it appears safe to say that they did. Paul says, "I am on my way to Jerusalem in the service of the saints there. For Macedonia and Achaia were pleased to make a contribution for the poor among the saints in Jerusalem" (Romans 15:26-27). God's word does not return to him empty. The word of God Paul brought to Corinth in these chapters was, as is all of God's word, powerful and effective.

"My grace is sufficient for you."

PART THREE: A LOOK TO THE FUTURE — PAUL SPEAKS OF HIS COMING VISIT TO CORINTH AND WHAT THIS IMPLIES FOR HIS ADVERSARIES (10:1-13:10)

We have come now to the third of the three major sections of 2 Corinthians. In the first section (chapters 1-7) Paul looked to the past. He explained why he had not come to Corinth directly from Ephesus as he had said he would. In the process of that explanation he extolled the praises of the ministry of the New Covenant. In the second section (chapters 8 and 9) Paul looked to the present, to the uncompleted offering for the church at Jerusalem. He urged the Corinthians to finish gathering it in and offered counsel and assistance to help bring it to completion.

Now, in the section before us, Paul looks to the immediate future. Within a short time, probably just a few months, he will be coming personally to Corinth. Before he does, he has a message for his adversaries there and for those who are listening to them. In this message he employs some stern words.

Though Paul could say to the Corinthians, "I have complete confidence in you" (2 Corinthians 7:16), that did not apply to every individual in the congregation. There were some, likely just a handful, in the church at Corinth who still bitterly opposed Paul and who were having an effect on a small minority of the congregation.

This is the issue he addresses in the final chapters of 2 Corinthians. That explains the abrupt change of tone between chapters nine and ten. The change is so marked, in fact, that some find it hard to accept that these chapters are part of the same letter. The difference in tone, however, is simply due to the difference in subject matter.

We can divide the final four chapters of 2 Corinthians into the following three sections:

- Paul's ministry compared with that of the "super-apostles" (10:1-11:15)
- Paul's boasts (11:16-12:13)
- Paul's coming third visit to Corinth (12:14-13:10)

Then follow some final greetings and a benediction.

PAUL'S MINISTRY COMPARED WITH THAT OF THE "SUPER-APOSTLES" (10:1-11:15)

Paul's Weapons

10 **By the meekness and gentleness of Christ, I appeal to you — I, Paul, who am "timid" when face to face with you, but "bold" when away! [2]I beg you that when I come I may not have to be as bold as I expect to be toward some people who think that we live by the standards of this world.**

Paul becomes very personal in these chapters, as can be seen by how often he uses the first person singular pronoun "I." In the previous chapters he had frequently used "we" instead of "I," often indicating by this that his co-workers were expressing the same sentiments. Here, however, it is Paul alone who is confronting his detractors and those who were lending them a willing ear.

We should not fail to note how evangelically Paul addresses those who have allowed themselves to be influenced by the slanderous statements of his opponents. He doesn't begin these chapters with, "I order you. . . . I command you." He says, "I *appeal* to you. . . . I *beg* you." This is brotherly admonition. He is addressing brothers and sisters in the faith, however weak they might be. His desire is to deal with them the way his Savior would have, with *meekness and gentleness*. In fact, Paul makes it clear that it is only *by the meekness and gentleness of Christ* that he is able to handle the situation in this manner. The Christ-like qualities of meekness and gentleness don't come naturally. They flow out of the hearts of those in whom Christ dwells.

It is clear that Paul's good name was being maligned by those who opposed him. They were maintaining that Paul was cowardly, that he was *bold* when he wrote letters to them from a distance (cf. verse 10), but that when he was face to face with the Corinthians, the *bold* Paul all of a sudden turned into a *timid,* cowardly Paul.

It is true that Paul had been quite bold when he had written to them. That letter had been what we today call 1 Corinthians. In 1 Corinthians Paul faced head-on the many problems in the congregation, the Corinthians' cliquishness, their quarreling, their moral laxity, their pride. Earlier in 2 Corinthians Paul had said, "I wrote as I did [in 1 Corinthians] so that when I came I should not be distressed by those who ought to make me rejoice" (2:3). His purpose had been to lead them to repentance. Then his next visit could be joyful both for him and the Corinthians.

Paul didn't want to have to be bold, a stern preacher of the law, when he came to Corinth. It looked, however, as though he would have to be just that toward some, the ones who were charging Paul with living *by the standards of this world*, literally, "according to the flesh." They were accusing him of catering to his sinful flesh, of being a politician in the worst sense of the word, of tailoring his speech and actions according to what would bring the most advantage to him.

Paul refutes this charge in no uncertain terms:

³For though we live in the world, we do not wage war as the world does.

Literally translated, Paul is saying, "Though we live *in* the flesh, we do not wage war *according to* the flesh." Paul was a human being. He lived "in the flesh." As a human being, he was not immune to the pressure his own sinful flesh would exert on him to deal with people in a "fleshly" way. If he allowed his flesh to dictate to him, he would do whatever it took to come out on top. He would be devious or underhanded. He would talk out of both sides of his mouth. He would try to bully people or smooth-talk people into submission — whatever "worked."

But that was not the way Paul operated. He would not *wage war* "according to the flesh." He had something much better to rely on than anything the flesh could come up with.

⁴The weapons we fight with are not the weapons of the world. On the contrary, they have divine power to demolish strongholds. ⁵We demolish arguments and every pretension that sets itself up against the knowledge of God, and we take captive every thought to make it obedient to Christ.

Again, the word the NIV translates as *of the world* literally means "of the flesh." As Paul confronts those who oppose him in Corinth, he will not put his stock in anything that originates in his flesh. Rather, he will look outside of himself to a weapon that has *divine power.* It is a weapon that is able

to *demolish strongholds . . . and arguments and every preten-*
sion that sets itself up against the knowledge of God.

In a word, this weapon is the gospel. That is all Paul needed as he came to Corinth. The gospel has the power to *de-*
molish strongholds, to destroy any opposition in its path.
This opposition may take the form of *arguments,* of human
reasoning that calls the message of the cross foolishness. It
may take the form of *pretension,* a haughty spirit that rejects
the need for a saving *knowledge of God* that comes from
faith in Christ.

When Paul came to Corinth, he would come armed with
just this one weapon, the gospel. That is the way he had
come to Corinth the first time. In 1 Corinthians he had reminded them:

> When I came to you, brothers, I did not come with
> eloquence or superior wisdom as I proclaimed to you
> the testimony about God. For I resolved to know noth-
> ing while I was with you except Jesus Christ and him
> crucified. I came to you in weakness and fear, and with
> much trembling. My message and my preaching were
> not with wise and persuasive words, but with a demon-
> stration of the Spirit's power, so that your faith might
> not rest on men's wisdom, but on God's power (2:1-5).

Paul is saying the same thing in these verses. The gospel
was all he needed. Paul was blessed with a great intellect,
which he had formerly used as an enemy of the gospel. By
God's grace, however, he had come to see that the gospel
was much more powerful than his strong intellect and much
wiser than any human argument he could devise.

He still used his intellect, but now he says, *We take captive*
every thought to make it obedient to Christ. He refused to let
his intellect run free, to allow it to become the servant of his

179

flesh, to use it for self-serving purposes. Now he used his intellect in the service of the gospel. He would come to Corinth, not relying on a razor-sharp mind, but on the even sharper sword of the Spirit, the gospel of Christ.

What the gospel had done in Paul's case was repeated wherever Paul proclaimed it. The gospel has within it the power to turn a person completely around. After a Christian is converted by the gospel, he will still use his mind, his intellect. Now, however, he will employ it to serve the gospel rather than to oppose it.

Christians today can learn from Paul. The unbelieving world is not going to be conquered for Christ through the use of human weapons, whether it be cleverly constructed programs or carefully concocted arguments. Mankind's problems are spiritual in nature. Only the word, the law to reveal sin, the gospel to shine the spotlight on the Savior, has the power to demolish human *strongholds, arguments,* and *pretensions,* the barriers people set up that prevent them from coming to a saving *knowledge of God.*

6And we will be ready to punish every act of disobedience, once your obedience is complete.

With these words Paul indicates that there are two different groups in Corinth needing his attention. The one group was that small number of individuals, "super-apostles" he calls them in chapter 11 (verse 5), who continued to slander Paul and thus the gospel he represented. The other group consisted of those who were listening to this slander and were in danger of being drawn away from Paul and the one message that saves.

Paul deals differently with each group. He is going to have to take some stern measures with the "super-apostles." He talks about being ready to *punish every act of disobedience.*

This, however, would not be Paul's first order of business when he arrived in Corinth. He would first turn his attention to the second group, those who were being influenced by the "super-apostles." He saw them as weak believers who needed personal pastoral care, believers whose *obedience* needed to be made *complete*. They were beginning to go astray. They needed gently to be shown the danger of listening to the wrong voices and then to be restored to the right path. After that Paul would turn his attention to the trouble-makers.

Paul's way of dealing with these two groups in Corinth is instructive for us. It serves as a reminder that when disciplining is called for, we must carefully differentiate between those who are weak in their faith and those who are stubbornly persisting in an ungodly action or belief. We need to deal gently with the weak as we call them to repentance and seek to restore them to the right path. Sterner measures, however, are called for when people willfully persist in their error.

One strategy doesn't fit all. In concern for the individual soul, we need to determine whom we are working with, the weak or the impenitent, and then conform our approach to the situation.

In the verses that follow Paul alerts the weak believers in Corinth to the fact that they are being led astray. He makes it clear that his opponents have been misreading his actions.

Paul's Consistency

7You are looking only on the surface of things. If anyone is confident that he belongs to Christ, he should consider again that we belong to Christ just as much as he.

It is probably better to take the first sentence of verse 7 as it is rendered in the footnote of the NIV: "Look at the obvious facts." In the original language it can be translated either way. It appears from the context, though, that Paul here is challenging the weak Corinthian believers to do something. They should look at things as they really are.

What are the obvious facts? *If anyone is confident that he belongs to Christ, he should consider again that we belong to Christ just as much as he.* What Paul means by this statement is not as obvious as we might like it to be. The difficulty in understanding this sentence revolves around the *anyone* he refers to. Whom does Paul have in mind here?

There are two possibilities. With *anyone* Paul could be referring to the "super-apostles." In this interpretation, he would be picturing these men as coming to Corinth and claiming special apostolic authority, saying, in effect, "Don't trust Paul. Trust us. We come right from Jerusalem." Paul brings out in chapter 11 that these "super-apostles" were doing just that, "masquerading as apostles of Christ" (verse 13).

If the *anyone* of this verse refers to the "super-apostles," Paul would be arguing: "Is someone coming to you claiming special authority for himself, saying that he is of Christ? Even if, for the sake of argument, we accept this claim, let that someone keep in mind that we are of Christ just as much as he is." Paul's point would be that the Corinthians should not let the claims of others cause them to forget that Paul himself came to them with all of the authority of an apostle.

Though a goodly number of commentators take the verse in this way, they fail to take into account the word the NIV translates with *is confident*. The *someone* Paul refers to is not portrayed as claiming, or telling others, that he belongs to Christ, but rather as being *confident* that he belongs to Christ. This refers to an inner certainty. In the following chapter Paul will bring out that the "super-apostles" could not be described as people who were confident that they belonged to Christ. They were hypocrites. They claimed to be that which they knew they were not.

It is, therefore, more probable that with the word *anyone* Paul is alluding to any of the Corinthian Christians who were in danger of being taken in by the "super-apostles." In that case Paul is saying something to this effect: "If you are confident that you are a Christian, you know what it means to be a Christian. You know that a Christian is one who trusts in Jesus Christ for the forgiveness of sins and a right standing in the eyes of God. Well, then, you should have no trouble recognizing that I, Paul, together with those who worked with me, men such as Titus and Timothy, are Christians also. Our confession of faith is the same as yours. In fact, the reason you can be confident that you are a Christian stems from the fact that we declared to you the message through which the Holy Spirit brought you to faith."

In this interpretation, Paul's point would be that the Corinthians should keep on listening to him since he was a Christian as they were. The unspoken, but certainly understood, conclusion would be that if both the Corinthians and Paul belonged to Christ, the Corinthians should be very wary of others who came with a message different from Paul's and who were critical of Paul's ministry. They should be suspect, not Paul.

With this reminder, that he, too, is of Christ, Paul takes up once again some of the charges of those who oppose him.

8For even if I boast somewhat freely about the authority the Lord gave us for building you up rather than pulling you down, I will not be ashamed of it.

Paul evidently was being accused of being too authoritarian, especially in his letters, of "pulling rank," so to speak.

He offers a two-fold response to this criticism. First, he was not brazenly assuming a position that did not belong to him. It was authority that *the Lord gave.* He was an apostle. An apostle was an authoritative spokesman for Christ. Paul had to speak and act with authority, or he would have been unfaithful to the one who had called him to faith and commissioned him to go out in his name.

Secondly, Paul tells the Corinthians, "I used this authority *for building you up rather than pulling you down.*" Paul's whole ministry, even when he used the law, always had the ultimate goal of building people up, not tearing them down. What he tore down were the strongholds of Satan, whatever kept people from a saving knowledge of Jesus or threatened their relationship with him.

In this Paul serves as a model for the way spiritual authority should be exercised, whether by parents in a Christian home or by pastors and other spiritual leaders in a congregation. For one thing, whatever authority the Lord has given to Christians should be put to use. It would not have been right for Paul to fail to employ his authority as an apostle when he saw the Corinthians getting into trouble. In the same way it is not proper today if parents or leaders in the church fail to use their spiritual authority when discipline is called for.

Secondly, spiritual leaders in the home and church can learn from Paul how to use their authority in a proper way. It should always have the ultimate purpose of building up, not tearing down. The purpose of discipline, whether in the Christian home or the church, is to train as a disciple, to bring about a closer walk with Jesus. The law will be needed to expose the sin that is preventing that walk. But the gospel is also required to assure forgiveness and to move God's child to follow gladly wherever his Savior leads.

⁹I do not want to seem to be trying to frighten you with my letters. ¹⁰For some say, "His letters are weighty and forceful, but in person he is unimpressive and his speaking amounts to nothing." ¹¹Such people should realize that what we are in our letters when we are absent, we will be in our actions when we are present.

In these words Paul is amplifying what he had said at the beginning of this chapter. There he had referred to the charge of his opponents that he was "bold" when he was away from them and "timid" when he was present. In the previous verse Paul had explained why he was bold in the letters he wrote when he could not be present with the Corinthians. Everything he had written had the purpose of building them up. It wasn't that he was *trying to frighten* them, even though the tone had to be somewhat stern.

Those who were seeking to push Paul aside in favor of themselves had seized on this sternness of tone to accuse Paul of being inconsistent: He was *weighty* and *forceful* in his letters, but in person he was *unimpressive,* literally, "weak." In fact, they said, *his speaking amounts to nothing.*

This charge apparently does not have so much to do with what Paul said when he was present with the Corinthians as with the manner of his appearance and speech. His physical appearance was not all that impressive, nor did he possess the kind of eloquence in speech that his opponents apparently displayed. Or, if he did, he didn't use it. Already in his first letter he had reminded the Corinthians that he had not come to them "with eloquence and wisdom," but rather "in weakness and fear, and with much trembling" (1 Corinthians 2:2). He had been and still was concerned that the Corinthians' faith would not "rest on men's wisdom" or rhetorical skills, but "on God's power" that came through the simple message of the gospel (1 Corinthians 2:5).

Paul's personal appearance and his manner of speech were, therefore, completely consistent with the way he wrote. In both cases, whether away from the Corinthians or present with them, he knew that it was the word alone, not his personality, that could touch the Corinthians' hearts. Only the word could produce repentance, assure forgiveness, and empower godly living.

It was, therefore, erroneous to charge Paul with being bold and brave when away and spineless when present. His opponents would soon discover first-hand how wrong they were to indict Paul in this way. *Such people* (the kind of people who make this charge) *should realize that what we are in our letters when we are absent,* that is, bold and powerful, *we will be in our actions when we are present.* The key words here are *letters* and *actions.* Paul was being criticized for being inconsistent. When he arrived in Corinth and confronted his accusers, they would learn the hard way how consistent Paul was. What he wrote he was going to do. If they had refused to listen to the law in his letters, they would have to be confronted with the same law when he arrived. As he had put it in a previous verse, when he came to Corinth, he would *be ready to punish every act of disobedience* (verse 6).

Paul's Standard of Measurement

12We do not dare to classify or compare ourselves with some who commend themselves. When they measure themselves by themselves and compare themselves with themselves, they are not wise.

The Corinthians should realize that those who were challenging Paul were using a faulty standard of measurement. *They measure themselves by themselves and compare themselves with themselves,* that is, by the standards they have set for themselves.

What were their standards? In their attempt to woo the Corinthians away from Paul, they would obviously point to those qualities they felt they possessed and Paul didn't. While Paul doesn't list their standards of measurement, a reading of the final chapters of 2 Corinthians does give us some clues as to what these "super-apostles" were boasting about. Evidently they were trained speakers, possessing superior oratorical skills; that was not Paul's strong suit (11:6). Possibly because of their skill, they considered it only right that they should receive remuneration for their work; the reason why Paul took nothing, so the charge would go, was that he had nothing of any value to give (11:7). They had an impeccable Hebrew ancestry; Paul wasn't even from Palestine (11:21,22). They were servants of Christ; Paul had been a persecutor of Christ (11:23).

In the next two chapters Paul will be refuting these arguments. At this point he simply asserts in a deliberate understatement that people who boast that they represent the Lord but then measure themselves by self-chosen standards *are not wise*.

13We, however, will not boast beyond proper limits, but will confine our boasting to the field God has assigned to us, a field that reaches even to you.

As Paul will bring out repeatedly in the next few chapters, he is being forced to boast about himself. This is very distasteful to him, but if he does not defend himself against the "super-apostles," some of the Corinthian believers might turn away from him and thereby turn to "a Jesus other than the Jesus" (11:4) Paul had preached to them.

Out of necessity, therefore, he is going to become a boaster, but he is not going to do as the "super-apostles" have done.

187

He is not going to set up his own standard of measurement and then boast about how well he has done. He is not going to boast "on the basis of things that don't serve as a standard of measurement," which is a somewhat more literal rendering of the phrase translated *beyond proper limits*. Measuring oneself by oneself does not serve as a proper standard of measurement.

How, then, does Paul measure himself? And how should the Corinthians determine if Paul is measuring up to what he should be doing? If, as he claims, he is a genuine apostle of Christ, that means he has received his commission, his "marching orders," from Christ. The Corinthians, then, should be evaluating Paul's ministry by how faithfully he has been carrying out his Christ-given commission. And, since the "super-apostles" also claim to be "servants of Christ" (11:23), they also should be measured by this standard.

The Corinthians should measure Paul and the "super-apostles" by a single standard: What is the commission they have received from Christ, and how faithfully are they carrying it out? If they do that, they will not be comparing apples and oranges, but will have a common, and reliable, basis for evaluation.

Having made that clear, Paul zeroes in on one specific feature of Christ's commission. He says, *We will confine our boasting to the field God has assigned to us, a field that reaches even to you.* To understand what Paul is saying here, we have to go back to the days right after his conversion. In Damascus the Lord appeared in a vision to Ananias, telling him about Saul of Tarsus, "This man is my chosen instrument to carry my name before the Gentiles and their kings and before the people of Israel" (Acts 9:15). It was to the Gentiles especially that Paul was to bring the gospel. The leaders in the Jerusalem church had recognized this. In Galatians Paul had written: "James, Peter and John . . . gave me and Barnabas the right hand of fellowship when they recognized the grace given to me. They agreed that we should go to the Gentiles, and they to the Jews" (Galatians 2:9).

By direct commission of Christ, Paul's ministry was to focus on the Gentile world. He would preach the gospel, as he puts it, "where Christ was not known, so that I would not be building on someone else's foundation" (Romans 15:20). That is why he had come to Corinth. His Christ-given field of responsibility, he tells the Corinthians, *reaches even to you;* for this was the Gentile world and a place where the gospel had not yet been preached.

Paul's point is a simple one: How can you Corinthians know if you should look upon me and my co-workers or upon the "super-apostles" as your legitimate spiritual leaders? Just ask yourselves whom Christ himself sent to you. It was we, not they.

It is true yet today that there is no legitimate service in the public ministry of the church apart from a call. In Paul's case that call had come directly from Christ upon the occasion of his conversion. Today the call into the public ministry generally comes through an assembly of believers who ask a properly qualified individual to carry on a ministry of word and sacrament in their name and on their behalf. For one to seek to assume such a position without a call puts him in that respect into the category of the "super-apostles" who in reality had called themselves to Corinth and set themselves up in opposition to Paul's legitimate, Christ-originated ministry.

[14]We are not going too far in our boasting, as would be the case if we had not come to you, for we did get as far as you with the gospel of Christ.

If Paul had not come to Corinth and brought them the gospel, he would have had no claim on their loyalty. But the fact is that he had come, faithfully fulfilling his commission as apostle to the Gentiles. The last part of this verse in the NIV translation doesn't quite pick up on another point that Paul is making in this verse. The NASB translation is preferable here: "We were the first to come even as far as you." Not only had Paul come to Corinth, he had arrived there and carried on his work there considerably in advance of the "super-apostles." "Measure me," says Paul, "by my faithfulness to what the Lord has commissioned me to do." Implied in this is the thought that the Corinthians would look in vain for a commission of Jesus to the "super-apostles" to come and "set up shop" right in the midst of Paul's field of labor. Paul didn't operate that way and neither should they.

15Neither do we go beyond our limits by boasting of work done by others. Our hope is that, as your faith continues to grow, our area of activity among you will greatly expand, 16so that we can preach the gospel in the regions beyond you. For we do not want to boast about work already done in another man's territory.

At the beginning of verse 15 Paul repeats what he has said in verse 13. He is going to be careful about the way he measures his ministry. He is not going to measure it by standards which are not a legitimate standard of measurement. Here, however, he is pointing to what his opponents had done. They had come to Corinth where Paul, over a period of one-and-a-half years, had carefully laid a sound gospel foundation. They had disrupted this work. They had thrown many people into turmoil. They had caused many to question Paul's integrity and Paul's message.

And in all this they evidently had been boasting that they, not Paul, were the dispensers of what the Corinthians really needed. This boasting was taking place where others had been laboring, where they had no call to be. By no proper standard of measurement could they claim to be faithful servants of Christ.

That was not Paul's method. His commission as apostle to the Gentiles, his call to bring the gospel where it had not yet been heard, was never far from his mind. One reason, in fact, he hopes he will be able to settle things in Corinth is that he would like to be able to move on from Corinth.

Paul states his hope in this way: *Our hope is that . . . our area of activity among you will greatly expand.* This is a somewhat difficult phrase in the original Greek. Putting it a little more literally, it could be translated: "We have the hope that, in keeping with our assignment and with your assistance, we might be greatly enlarged."

Not only does Paul hope that his ministry will be enlarged, or expanded, to areas beyond Corinth. He also hopes that the Corinthians will be able to assist him with this work. This assistance could come in various ways. They could pray for him as he moved on to new areas. They could perhaps help him financially. Possibly some of them could even accompany Paul. But all of this was contingent on settling matters in Corinth. *As your faith continues to grow,* Paul tells the Corinthians, then I will be able to move elsewhere and also enlist your support.

This is a reminder that outreach and nurture go hand in hand. One cannot exist without the other. As Christians grow in faith, nurtured by word and sacrament, they are thereby also being motivated and equipped to assist in bringing the gospel to others.

Paul wants to *preach the gospel in the regions beyond* Corinth. If things settled down in Corinth, he could use it as his base of operations to head west. That, apparently, is what did occur. In his letter to the Romans, written from Corinth a few months after the writing of 2 Corinthians, Paul tells the Romans that his work in Achaia, where Corinth was located, and in Macedonia was complete and that he planned to visit Rome on the way to Spain (cf. Romans 15:19-24).

Because there was already a congregation in Rome, he would not remain there long. This was in keeping with his apostolic commission: *We do not want to boast about work already done in another man's territory.* With these words Paul is once again pointing to a key difference between the "super-apostles" and himself. He has been measuring his ministry by what the Lord has commissioned him to do. In that he can boast. The "super-apostles," with their intrusion into *another man's territory,* are boasting about work they have taken into their own hands, without any authorization from the Lord. About that they have no right to boast.

¹⁷But, "Let him who boasts boast in the Lord."

The idea of boasting about one's labors was completely foreign to Paul. It made him uneasy to do this, as will be brought out even more clearly in the two chapters that follow. Some years before this he had emphatically told the Galatians, "May I never boast except in the cross of our Lord Jesus Christ" (Galatians 6:14). He knew that in this situation, however, he had no choice. If some of the Corinthians rejected Paul, they would also reject the gospel Paul preached.

He closes this chapter with a quotation from the Old Testament which will help to keep before the minds of the Corinthians the reason for Paul's boasting. He is quoting from the words of the Lord recorded by the prophet Jeremiah:

This is what the Lord says: "Let not the wise man boast of his wisdom or the strong man boast of his strength or the rich man boast of his riches, but let him who boasts boast about this: that he understands and knows me, that I am the Lord, who exercises kindness, justice and righteousness on earth, for in these I delight" (Jeremiah 9:23,24).

That is the kind of spirit in which Paul boasts. His boast is *in the Lord.* He has simply endeavored to show that his ministry has been clearly in line with the Lord's commission. That, of course, is what really counts.

18For it is not the one who commends himself who is approved, but the one whom the Lord commends.

With these words Paul brings to a conclusion the subject he began in verse 12 where he talked about those who "commend themselves" and "compare themselves with themselves." Anyone can commend himself for living up to standards he has set for himself. What the true believer looks for, however, is the "well-done, good and faithful servant" spoken by his or her Lord.

In his first letter, Paul had told the Corinthians, "It is required that those who have been given a trust must prove faithful" (1 Corinthians 4:2). When he looked back on his ministry in Corinth, Paul could confidently claim, "By the grace of God I have been faithful to the trust he has given to me. Measure me by that and you will see the folly of following those whose only ground for boasting is that they measure themselves by themselves."

Christians today also can take comfort in the fact that our Lord never expects more than faithfulness to what he has called us to do. And even when we falter in our faithfulness, the forgiveness won by Christ on Calvary is there to cleanse and restore to a more faithful walk.

Paul's Claims on the Corinthians' Loyalty

11 I hope you will put up with a little of my foolishness; but you are already doing that.

Paul uses the word *foolishness* to describe the boasting he had felt compelled to do in chapter ten. What he had spoken in this chapter, of course, could in no way be labelled "foolishness." He had established clearly how his work in Corinth had been in line with the commission Christ himself had given to him.

Rather, with the word *foolishness* Paul is thinking of the manner in which he had felt compelled to write. It was unlike Paul to boast about anything connected with himself. This was not the Paul the Corinthians had come to know during his one-and-a-half years in Corinth. The magnitude of the problem in Corinth, however, required this untypical approach.

In the next few verses Paul is going to demonstrate that his concern runs much deeper than a simple, "Whom do you want as your leader, Paul or the 'super-apostles'?" It was rather a matter of a real Jesus or a counterfeit Jesus, a real gospel or a counterfeit gospel. If it takes resorting to such "foolishness" as boasting about the legitimacy of his ministry to keep the Corinthians loyal to the real Jesus and the real gospel, then Paul is ready to do it.

2I am jealous for you with a godly jealousy. I promised you to one husband, to Christ, so that I might present you as a pure virgin to him.

Paul's motives were pure. He looked upon his ministry in the way John the Baptist had looked upon his. When John was informed that everyone was flocking to Jesus, he responded,

> The bride belongs to the bridegroom. The friend who attends the bridegroom waits and listens for him, and is full of joy when he hears the bridegroom's voice. That joy is mine, and it is now complete. He must become greater; I must become less (John 3:29,30).

John's main purpose as the friend of the Bridegroom, Jesus, was to bring his bride, the Church, to him. Having done that, John's mission was complete.

Using a somewhat similar picture, Paul portrays himself as the father of the bride. He had been a spiritual father to the believers in Corinth. As their "father" he had found a perfect "husband" for them, the one husband who could give them everything they needed for this life and the next. Through Paul's gospel preaching the Holy Spirit had awakened faith in the Corinthians' hearts, and through that they had become betrothed to Christ.

I promised [betrothed] *you to one husband, to Christ,* says Paul, *so that I might present you as a pure virgin to him.* With these last words Paul is looking ahead to the last day, when the Bridegroom comes to take his bride home with him. Paul's concern is that the Corinthians will be ready to meet him. His prayer is that he can present them to the Bridegroom as a *pure virgin,* that they will still be looking to Christ and him alone as their hope and Savior.

The intrusion of the "super-apostles" was endangering the bridegroom/bride relationship the Corinthians were enjoying with Christ and thus also threatening their readiness on the day of the Bridegroom's coming. Paul brings this out in the

195

verses that follow. Having stated that he wants to be able to present the Corinthians as a *pure virgin* to their Bridegroom, Christ, at his coming, Paul says:

³But I am afraid that just as Eve was deceived by the serpent's cunning, your minds may somehow be led astray from your sincere and pure devotion to Christ.

With these words Paul is getting to the heart of the problem. The Corinthians were being *led astray* from *their sincere and pure devotion to Christ*. If the situation didn't change, they were in grave danger of forsaking the Bridegroom altogether. Then they would not be ready when he returned to claim his bride, the Church.

What was causing this to happen? The Corinthians were being deceived, just as Eve had been *deceived by the serpent's cunning*.

⁴For if someone comes to you and preaches a Jesus other than the Jesus we preached, or if you receive a different spirit from the one you received, or a different gospel from the one you accepted, you put up with it easily enough.

In the way the original Greek puts it, the word "if" at the beginning of this verse does not convey a sense of uncertainty. This is something that is actually happening. Somebody is coming, says Paul, and preaching *a Jesus other than the Jesus we preached*. Notice that Paul does not say, as he could say about himself, that this someone was sent by Christ. All he says is that he comes. He is referring to the "super-apostles" with their self-appointed ministry.

In this verse Paul is adding another thought to the one he had developed in the previous chapter. Not only had these men come to Corinth without a proper call, they had also come without a proper message. The Jesus they were preaching was not the Jesus Paul had preached.

This points to the deceptive nature of their message. They had not denied the existence of Jesus. They had probably also affirmed that he was the Messiah. In some critical way, however, they had distorted the truth about Jesus. They had brought to Corinth a *different spirit* and a *different gospel,* not like the gospel the Corinthians had welcomed when Paul had been in their midst. This was a critical matter, for, as Paul had written to the Galatians, a "different gospel" is "really no gospel at all" (Galatians 1:6,7).

We cannot state with certainty what this "other Jesus" and "different spirit" and "different gospel" were, since Paul does not go into detail. We can, however, be safe in saying that the message of the "super-apostles" in some way would have robbed the Corinthians of the assurance that their standing with God was due one hundred pecent to the substitutionary work of Jesus on their behalf.

That kind of a "gospel," which was not the gospel at all, would produce a *different spirit* in the Corinthians. The real gospel results in freedom, in certainty, in hope, in joy, in peace. A counterfeit gospel keeps a person enslaved. It engenders a spirit of fear and uncertainty. It cannot produce true peace of heart and mind. It cannot give one the kind of inner joy that can confidently assert, "All is right between me and God; therefore, whatever the circumstances, I can be content."

A *different gospel* provides no certainty of one's standing with God now or on the day of judgment. Souls were therefore at stake. It should come as no surprise, then, that Paul should devote such a large percentage of 2 Corinthians to defending his ministry, a ministry that had brought to the Corinthians the real Jesus and the real gospel. It is also quite understandable why he should be exerting so much energy in combatting his opponents, who had brought in this counterfeit "gospel" and had done it in such a deceptive manner that some of the Corinthians were being taken in by it.

Deception is the mark yet today of those who come with another Jesus and a different spirit and gospel. As Jesus said, false prophets come "in sheep's clothing" (Matthew 7:15). They don't advertise themselves for what they are. Christians today need to look beneath the surface of those who may name the name of Jesus and speak of the "gospel." They should make sure they are speaking of the Jesus of the Scriptures and are proclaiming a gospel that points to Jesus as the one who has done everything that is necessary for a right standing with God in this life and the next.

⁵But I do not think I am in the least inferior to those "super-apostles." ⁶I may not be a trained speaker, but I do have knowledge. We have made this perfectly clear to you in every way.

In the previous verse Paul had told the Corinthians, *You put up with it,* that is, with the false message of the intruders, *easily enough.* That comes as somewhat of a surprise to Paul because, as he puts it in a deliberate under-statement, he doesn't consider himself to be *in the least inferior to those "super-apostles."* Why, then, should the Corinthians be so quick to turn to the intruders?

This is the first time he has used the term "super-apostles." He still doesn't name these men, and he won't do that anywhere in the letter. He doesn't intend to dignify them and their false message by displaying their names. The Corinthians know who they are. That is not the problem.

The problem is that they are listening to them. That is why Paul reminds the Corinthians that he isn't inferior to these men. They were trained speakers and Paul wasn't? What difference did that make? What counted was that Paul possessed *knowledge*. He knew the truth. And what he knew he had *made perfectly clear* to the Corinthians *in every way*. Paul is probably referring here to his eighteen months of gospel ministry in Corinth.

If the message of the "super-apostles" was different from Paul's, it was their message that left something to be desired, not Paul's, no matter how far they may have surpassed Paul in speaking ability. What is said is of greater importance than how eloquently it is being spoken.

That is true in our time also, of course. Christians should judge those who come with the word by the content of their message. A gifted, persuasive speaker is not necessarily an authentic preacher of the gospel.

Paul's Non-Mercenary Motives

7Was it a sin for me to lower myself in order to elevate you by preaching the gospel of God to you free of charge? 8I robbed other churches by receiving support from them so as to serve you. 9And when I was with you and needed something, I was not a burden to anyone, for the brothers who came from Macedonia supplied what I needed. I have kept myself from being a burden to you in any way, and will continue to do so.

With these words Paul is apparently taking up another charge hurled against him by his opponents. It stemmed from the fact that Paul would accept no money for his services from the Corinthians. He had preached the gospel to them *free of charge*. In order to *elevate* the Corinthians, to lift them up from the depths of sin and its curse, death, Paul had felt it necessary to *lower,* or humble, himself.

Paul is likely referring here to the time he spent in manual labor while he was carrying on his Corinthian ministry.

Shortly after his arrival in Corinth he had come into contact with Aquila and Priscilla. Luke tells us that "Paul went to see them, and because he was a tentmaker as they were, he stayed and worked with them. Every Sabbath he reasoned in the synagogue, trying to persuade Jews and Greeks" (Acts 18:2-4). Here was the original "tentmaker" ministry. Paul supported himself by working at the trade he had learned in his youth and in this way could preach the gospel *free of charge* to the Corinthians.

In addition to the money he had earned through tent-making, Paul had also received supplementary financial support from the congregations in Macedonia. He tells the Corinthians, *I robbed other churches by receiving support from them so as to serve you.* This was "robbery" only in the sense that the churches in Macedonia were very poor and therefore didn't have all that much money to spare. Yet Paul was willing to accept their gracious gifts so that he would not be a *burden* to the Corinthians *in any way.* That was the way Paul had operated when he had first come to Corinth, and, he says, *I . . . will continue to do so.*

This seemed to be the best approach, the one least likely to put a barrier between Paul and those he desired to serve. There were those in Paul's time, as there are yet today, who were bent on financially exploiting people in the name of religion. Paul had taken great pains so as not to be identified with them. He would work with his hands to put food on his table. He would accept gifts from those who had been brought to faith through his ministry. He would not, however, take anything from those to whom he was bringing the gospel for the first time. He wanted it to be clear that his motives were totally non-mercenary.

It seems as though Paul's opponents, the "super-apostles," had turned this very commendable approach of Paul into something entirely different. To the Greek mind manual labor, such as tentmaking, was undignified, hardly befitting a teacher and scholar. The fact that Paul is engaged in tentmaking, his opponents would say, should tell you something about him. He is just a common laborer, hardly the kind of person who deserves your respect. It is obvious why he isn't taking any money from you while we are: We have something of value to give you and he doesn't. You get what you pay for.

How does Paul respond to this charge?

10As surely as the truth of Christ is in me, nobody in the regions of Achaia will stop this boasting of mine. 11Why? Because I do not love you? God knows I do!

At the end of verse 9 Paul asserted that in Corinth he was going to continue to follow the policy of accepting no remuneration. In verse 10 he repeats this assertion in a passionate manner. He invokes the name of Christ to back up his contention: *As surely as the truth of Christ is in me, nobody in the regions of Achaia,* the province in which Corinth was located, *will stop this boasting of mine,* this boasting that he is bringing the gospel free of charge to the Corinthians.

One might be inclined to ask why Paul would not by this time be willing to accept support from the Corinthians. After all, he has just told them that he had accepted financial assistance from the believers in Macedonia. The Corinthians were believers also. Why should Paul operate by different standards with them than with the Macedonians?

Could it be that Paul didn't love the Corinthians as much as he loved the believers in the churches in Macedonia? Did he feel closer to the Macedonians and, therefore, more comfortable in receiving help from them? That, apparently, is what some of the Corinthians had concluded: Paul doesn't love them. Paul responds to this mistaken notion with an emphatic, *God knows I do!*

Why, then, would he not treat them in the same way as he had the Macedonians? This is his answer:

¹²And I will keep on doing what I am doing in order to cut the ground from under those who want an opportunity to be considered equal with us in the things they boast about.

Paul will keep on doing what he had been doing, he will keep on preaching the gospel to the Corinthians free of charge, because to do otherwise would be to play right into the hands of the "super-apostles." Though, as the previous verses indicate, the "super-apostles" evidently had been inferring that Paul was hardly worth listening to because he didn't ask for any money, they knew this was a rather weak argument. Paul could very well counter that claim with the argument, "Whom should you trust? Those who are taking from you or those who are giving to you?"

It would be better for the "super-apostles," therefore, if both Paul and they were *considered equal,* that is, if they were operating in the same way, in this matter of receiving or not receiving remuneration. There were two options. One alternative would be for the "super-apostles" to change their tactics and no longer accept any money from the Corinthians. That they were unwilling to do.

The other possibility would be for Paul to begin to accept gifts from the Corinthians as the "super-apostles" were doing. That Paul refuses to do. He will keep on carrying out his ministry free of charge *to cut the ground from under those who want an opportunity to be considered equal* with Paul in this matter. If they are really sincere, then let them, with

Paul, refuse to accept any remuneration. Paul wasn't going to lose any sleep worrying that they might decide to do that. It is in the nature of false prophets to peddle their wares as "a means to financial gain" (1 Timothy 6:5).

In these verses Paul gives us a good example of the proper use of Christian freedom. In 1 Corinthians he had clearly brought out that he had the right in God's eyes to receive financial compensation from the Corinthians (cf. 1 Corinthians 9:3-18). He had not used that right, however, when he had first come to Corinth, nor was he going to avail himself of it at this time. He had looked at the situation in Corinth and concluded that the cause of the gospel would be hindered if he did what he was entitled to do as a minister of the gospel.

Christians today also will be willing to limit their freedom for the sake of the gospel. They will not want to exercise that freedom, in whatever form it might take, if by doing so they would be setting up a barrier between themselves and those they are seeking to reach with the gospel.

Paul's Opponents Unmasked

¹³For such men are false apostles, deceitful workmen, masquerading as apostles of Christ.

Paul could not get any more blunt than this. The "super-apostles" were anything but that. They were not "super" and they were not "apostles." They were *false apostles,* who were *masquerading* as apostles of Christ. They were *deceitful workmen,* pretending to be one thing when they were actually something else. *False, deceitful, masquerading —* these three words describe the way false prophets operate. What you see is not what you get. Like the wolf in sheep's clothing, they disguise themselves to cover up what they are really like.

203

14And no wonder, for Satan himself masquerades as an angel of light. 15It is not surprising, then, if his servants masquerade as servants of righteousness. Their end will be what their actions deserve.

It should come as no surprise that false teachers masquerade as true teachers. In so doing they are following their master, Satan. From the beginning of time Satan has been the master masquerader. What he told Eve in the garden sounded logical, plausible, even wise. The truth was the opposite.

In labelling the self-styled "super-apostles" *false apostles,* Paul is setting an either-or situation before the Corinthians. They cannot follow both them and Paul. That would be like trying to follow Satan and God at the same time.

If Satan and his agents are masters at masquerading, how could the Corinthians and how can Christians today recognize them? In his Sermon on the Mount Jesus said, "By their fruit you will recognize them" (Matthew 7:16). The "fruit" of one who claims to be a *servant of righteousness* will be what comes out of his mouth, his teaching.

How does one know what teaching to accept and what to reject? The key is found in this word *righteousness.* Satan and those whom he is leading want people to believe that "righteousness," achieving a right standing with God, is at least partly their own doing. The name of Christ may be mentioned. He may even be called "Savior." But when all is said and done, Christ is pushed to the side and "righteousness" becomes a matter of self-attainment.

Like the Judaizers in Galatia, the "super-apostles" in Corinth were telling people that faith in Christ alone was not enough to assure them of a right standing with God. *Their end,* the end of such who masqueraded as God's servants but taught the message of Satan, *will be what their actions de-*

serve. If they believed what they taught, what awaited them at the end of time was not the Lord's "Well done, good and faithful servant" (Matthew 25:21), but his "Depart from me ... into the eternal fire prepared for the devil and his angels" (Matthew 25:41) and all who follow his lies.

A genuine *servant of righteousness,* on the other hand, will direct people to Christ and Christ alone for a right standing with God. This is the primary touchstone, that which divides Satan and his agents from true servants of righteousness. "If this doctrine [of righteousness through Christ alone] is lost," Luther writes, "it is impossible for us to be able to resist any errors or sects" (*Luther's Works,* vol. 26, p. 176).

Servants of righteousness need to proclaim the righteousness that comes by Christ, who lived a holy, righteous life in the place of unrighteous sinners and then died the death that sinners deserve. In him we "become the righteousness of God" (2 Corinthians 5:21).

PAUL'S BOASTS
(11:16-12:13)

Paul's Plea to Permit Foolish Boasting

¹⁶I repeat: Let no one take me for a fool. But if you do, then receive me just as you would a fool, so that I may do a little boasting. ¹⁷In this self-confident boasting I am not talking as the Lord would, but as a fool. ¹⁸Since many are boasting in the way the world does, I too will boast.

At the beginning of this chapter Paul had told the Corinthians, "I hope you will put up with a little of my foolishness" (11:1). He now returns to that thought, adding that he hopes the Corinthians won't consider him personally to be a fool, even if he speaks the way a fool does.

Paul knows that with what he is about to say he runs the risk of being labelled just that, a fool. That is why he adds, *If you do [take me for a fool], then receive me just as you would a fool, so that I might do a little boasting.* "Please bear with me," he is saying, "although I know this isn't the Paul you are used to hearing." He is quick to admit, in fact, that in what he is about to say he is *not talking as the Lord would.* A servant of the Lord normally would not boast as Paul has been doing in these chapters and is about to do in an even more noticeable manner in the verses that follow.

The circumstances, however, have compelled him to step out of character and to say, *I too will boast,* even as his opponents were doing. They were boasting about themselves *in the way the world does,* literally, "according to the flesh," as in 10:2-4. They were being led by their sinful flesh, boasting about whatever they thought might impress the Corinthians: their nationality, their birthplace, their training, their position, their extensive labors, the hardships they had endured.

And the Corinthians, at least some of them, were being taken in by this.

¹⁹You gladly put up with fools since you are so wise!

These words are laced with irony. Already in 1 Corinthians Paul had taken the Corinthians to task for boasting about their wisdom (cf. 1 Corinthians 4:10). Now he points to an example of how wise they really were: they *gladly put up with fools.* They had allowed themselves to be impressed by the outer wrappings of the "super-apostles," never bothering to look inside the package.

Paul mentions five things the "super-apostles" were doing to the Corinthians, all of which the "wise" Corinthians failed to see:

²⁰In fact, you even put up with anyone who enslaves you or exploits you or takes advantage of you or pushes himself forward or slaps you in the face.

The "super-apostles" were enslaving the Corinthians. This is probably a reference to the fact that they were preaching a different Jesus and a different gospel from the one Paul had preached. They were turning the Corinthians away from a gospel of full and free salvation to a salvation dependent at least to a degree on obedience to various ceremonial laws. By this they were putting the Corinthians into bondage all over again after they had been set free through the real gospel Paul had preached.

Secondly, the "super-apostles" were exploiting the Corinthians, literally, "devouring" them, "milking them dry," we might say. They were after their money, and the "wise" Corinthians meekly gave whatever they were told to give.

Thirdly, the Corinthians were being taken advantage of, literally, "taken in," deceived, duped by those who passed themselves off for what they were not.

The "super-apostles" were doing a fourth thing: They were pushing themselves forward, that is, putting on airs, acting in a proud and arrogant manner. Finally, they were even slapping the Corinthians in the face. This could mean that the Corinthians were permitting themselves to be physically mistreated by the "super-apostles." It is more likely, however, that by this Paul is referring to verbal abuse being inflicted on the Corinthians by these teachers who were seeking to take Paul's place.

It is not a pretty picture. The "super-apostles" come, haughty and arrogant, greedy and malicious, bent on taking advantage of the Corinthians for their own personal gain. And some of the Corinthians are allowing themselves to be exploited and tyrannized by these men.

21To my shame I admit that we were too weak for that!

These words, of course, are also being spoken in an ironical manner. "I'm sorry," Paul says, "that I haven't exploited you or taken advantage of you. I'm sorry for not being as 'strong' in this matter as the 'super-apostles.' I'm sorry for appearing to be 'weak' because I haven't ruled over you with an iron fist."

Earlier in this letter Paul had reminded the Corinthians, "Not that we lord it over your faith" (1:24). "We do not preach ourselves," he had told them, "but Jesus Christ as

Lord, and ourselves as your servants for Jesus' sake" (4:5). He was a "servant." As far as he was concerned, there was only one "Lord" and that was Jesus.

If the Corinthians wanted strength as the world looks at strength, they would have to turn elsewhere. But what a sad exchange it would be: the "super-apostles" as "lord" instead of Jesus Christ as Lord.

How could any of the Corinthians have been taken in so easily by these "super-apostles"? There was undoubtedly an appealing charisma about them. Their message would have had a certain ring of truth to it. In some way they would have promised their followers something better than what Paul was giving them. No different from the tactics of the serpent in the Garden of Eden! And no different from the tactics of seductive cult leaders today. They promise to give. In reality their purpose is to enslave, to exploit, to domineer.

True preachers of the gospel, with Paul, will always be too "weak" for such devious tactics. As servants of Jesus, their promise and their purpose will always be identical: to give people Jesus.

Paul's Trials

What anyone else dares to boast about — I am speaking as a fool — I also dare to boast about.

In verse 16 Paul had asked the Corinthians for permission to "do a little boasting." In the verses that followed he had explained why he felt it necessary to do this boasting, even if through this action the Corinthians should take him for a fool. The Corinthians were allowing themselves to be impressed by the kinds of credentials the world admires, credentials the "super-apostles" maintained they possessed and Paul lacked.

209

In the verses before us Paul takes the "super-apostles" on in their own arena. He sets before the Corinthians the kind of credentials his opponents were bragging about and demonstrates that his credentials are even more impressive than theirs. *What anyone else dares to boast about,* he says, *I also dare to boast about.*

But, he reminds them one more time, *I am speaking as a fool.* He would rather be talking about something else, but the Corinthians' infatuation with the "super-apostles" necessitates his boasting. It is not a matter of one-upmanship, but of defending the integrity of the gospel which had come from his lips.

We might add that, though Paul found it difficult to talk about himself in the way he does in the verses that follow, we are thereby given a fascinating glimpse into some of Paul's activities and experiences not mentioned anywhere else. Included among them is his "thorn in the flesh" experience in chapter 12, which has been a source of strength to many suffering Christians over the centuries.

22Are they Hebrews? So am I. Are they Israelites? So am I. Are they Abraham's descendants? So am I.

With these words Paul begins his boasting. Notice that his point is not to deny what the "super-apostles" were saying about themselves. It is rather, "If they can boast about that, so can I."

The "super-apostles" were bragging that they were *Hebrews, Israelites,* and *Abraham's descendants.* Although there may be some minor differences among these three terms, they are essentially speaking of the same thing. Paul's opponents were evidently insinuating that they were true Hebrews, Israelites, and descendants of Abraham and that, therefore, they were bringing a more pure form of Christianity to the Corinthians than Paul had. "Who is this Paul?" they would have argued. "He doesn't represent the Jerusalem establishment, which is the heart and center of the church, a church that sprang up out of Judaism. Paul, brought up hundreds of miles away in a Gentile community, Tarsus of Cilicia, is an outsider. He doesn't have the kind of understanding that we possess. He hasn't brought you a complete gospel."

To that Paul responds, "I too am a Hebrew." "A Hebrew of Hebrews," Paul calls himself in Philippians, "of the people of Israel" (cf. Philippians 3:5). He could trace his ancestry all the way back to Benjamin, one of the twelve sons of Jacob, and was thus no less a Hebrew, an Israelite, a descendant of Abraham than the "super-apostles."

Paul could have said more, of course, as he did in some of his other letters, to prove that he, not the "super-apostles," was a true Israelite and a true descendant of Abraham. In his letter to the Romans Paul states, "Not all who are descended from Israel are Israel. Nor because they are his descendants are they all Abraham's children" (Romans 9:6,7). The real Israelites, the real descendants of Abraham, are "those who have faith," those who "belong to Christ," Paul tells the Galatians (Galatians 3:9,29).

That, however, is not Paul's intent here. He is bringing out just one point. He is saying to the Corinthians, "You are impressed by a person's pedigree? Let me tell you that my family tree is no less impressive than that of those who have been boasting to you about theirs."

²³Are they servants of Christ? (I am out of my mind to talk like this.) I am more. I have worked much harder, been in prison more frequently, been flogged more severely, and been exposed to death again and again.

Do the "super-apostles" claim that they are ministers of Christ, that they are working hard and sacrificing much in his service? They have no idea what it means to serve, to labor, to sacrifice, says Paul. He then provides a catalog of his labors in the name of Jesus that make it clear he was much more a servant of Christ in this respect than the "super-apostles" were. But before doing that, he apologizes once again: *I am out of my mind to talk like this.* If that is what it took to impress the Corinthians, however, he would go on, no matter how personally distasteful it was for him to do it.

Not only had Paul worked hard, he had *worked much harder* than the "super-apostles." In 1 Corinthians Paul had mentioned how strenuously he had labored in his ministry. There, however, he had immediately added, "Yet not I, but the grace of God that was with me" (1 Corinthians 15:10). That was more in keeping with the character of Paul. He was always quick to give all glory to God.

Paul doesn't speak that way here, though, because it is not the point he is trying to get across. His opponents have been measuring their worth by looking at externals only. Paul is "playing their game." If they had worked hard, so had he — and more.

He had *been in prison more frequently.* Up to the writing of 2 Corinthians, the book of Acts records only one imprisonment of Paul, in Philippi with Silas (Acts 16:23-40). One of the early church fathers, Clement of Rome, writes that Paul was imprisoned seven different times. What Paul relates about his experiences here and in the verses that follow make it clear that Acts does not record everything that happened to Paul from the time of his conversion in the early 30s until his death in the mid- to late-60s.

Paul had been *flogged more severely* and had been *exposed to death again and again.* He goes into more detail in the verses that follow.

²⁴Five times I received from the Jews the forty lashes minus one. ²⁵Three times I was beaten with rods, once I was stoned, three times I was shipwrecked, I spent a night and a day in the open sea.

When Jesus sent out his disciples with the gospel, he forewarned them, "I am sending you out like sheep among wolves. . . . Be on your guard against men; they will hand you over to the local councils and flog you in their synagogues" (Matthew 10:16,17). Paul had been among the persecutors Jesus had warned his disciples about. He had gone "from one synagogue to another to imprison and beat" those who believed in Jesus (Acts 22:19).

After his conversion Paul found himself on the receiving end of similar beatings. *Five times* he had received from the Jews the *forty lashes minus one,* the maximum number allowed by Jewish law (cf. Deuteronomy 25:3). None of these beatings are mentioned in Acts.

Three times Paul had been *beaten with rods,* probably a reference to beatings he had received at the hands of government officials. One such beating is recorded in Acts, when he, a Roman citizen, was illegally beaten while imprisoned in Philippi (cf. Acts 16:23,37).

Paul mentions that once he had been *stoned.* The first mention of Paul in the Bible is connected with a stoning, that of Stephen. "Saul [later called Paul] was there," we are told, "giving approval to his death" (Acts 8:1). In Lystra on his first missionary journey Paul himself was almost stoned to death. Hostile Jews from nearby Iconium and Antioch stirred up the people in Lystra to attack him. They stoned him and then dragged him out of the city, leaving him for dead (cf. Acts 14:19).

Three times, says Paul, *I was shipwrecked, I spent a night and a day in the open sea.* The book of Acts tells us of only one shipwreck experience of Paul, and that occurred on his final voyage to Rome, more than two years after the writing of 2 Corinthians. Acts does record a number of sea voyages Paul made, however, prior to the time when 2 Corinthians was written. To spend a night and a day in the open sea, praying for another ship to sail close enough to see him and rescue him, this is yet another example of what Paul meant when he said that he had been exposed to death in his ministry.

26I have been constantly on the move. I have been in danger from rivers, in danger from bandits, in danger from my own countrymen, in danger from Gentiles; in danger in the city, in danger in the country, in danger at sea; and in danger from false brothers.

In his ministry Paul had been *constantly on the move.* During the ten years preceding the writing of 2 Corinthians, he had undertaken three extensive missionary journeys. He had traveled through much of the Roman provinces of Galatia, Asia, Macedonia, and Achaia. Wherever he had gone, he had faced *danger.*

In some cases Paul encountered dangers in nature. In his travels he often had to ford swiftly moving *rivers* and to sail on turbulent *seas.* In other cases the dangers Paul faced were caused by people. They came from *bandits* ready to pounce on an unarmed traveller. They emanated from his *own countrymen,* fellow Jews, who vigorously opposed his gospel ministry almost every place he went. The dangers Paul faced were also at times at the hands of the *Gentiles,* such as those who had him beaten in Philippi.

In the city . . . in the country . . . at sea, in other words, wherever he went, Paul faced dangers. He truly had been *exposed to death again and again.*

He mentions the most critical *danger* at the end: *in danger from false brothers.* Here the danger wasn't to the physical life of Paul but to the spiritual life of Paul's converts. Writing to the Galatians, Paul uses this same term "false brothers" (2:4) to describe those who had infiltrated the ranks in order to rob the Galatians of their freedom and make them slaves all over again. The same thing was happening in Corinth.

The dangers to his body Paul could accept. That was a problem only of this life. His earthly body would soon be gone and be replaced with a perfect heavenly body. The false brothers, however, endangered the eternal life of Paul's converts. That threat had to be overcome. That is precisely why Paul had been doing this uncharacteristic boasting. He would do whatever it took to keep the Corinthians from turning away from him to these *false brothers.*

Paul goes on with his boasting to make it clear that he is every bit the equal of the "super-apostles," and then some.

27I have labored and toiled and have often gone without sleep; I have known hunger and thirst and have often gone without food; I have been cold and naked.

The words *labored and toiled* serve as a general heading for this verse. Paul's ministry had been marked by labor and toil. This is undoubtedly, at least partially, a reference to his manual labor as a tent-maker. He used the same Greek words when writing to the Thessalonians, "We worked night and day, laboring and toiling so that we would not be a burden to any of you" (2 Thessalonians 3:8). Paul had not only gone without sleep in order to keep food on his table. At times he had preached the gospel late into the night, when others were free from their labors to be able to gather around the Word (cf. Acts 20:7-11,31).

Paul had *known hunger and thirst*. He had *often gone without food* and had been *cold and naked*, or ill-clothed. Though he was able to earn an income through his tent-making skills and though he had received a certain amount of help from the brothers and sisters in Macedonia, that apparently had not always covered all his physical needs.

When he wrote to the Philippians a few years after the writing of 2 Corinthians, Paul said, "I know what it is to be in need" (Philippians 4:12). With these words he wasn't complaining, however. He went on to say, "I have learned the secret of being content in any and every situation, whether well-fed or hungry, whether living in plenty or in want. I can do everything through him who gives me strength" (Philippians 4:12,13).

Neither was Paul complaining as he wrote to the Corinthians. He simply wanted them to know that the "super-apostles" had nothing up on him. Even if the Corinthians would judge him purely by such external standards as, "Who has worked the hardest? Who has sacrificed the most?", it would be no contest. Paul was the hands-down winner.

28Besides everything else, I face daily the pressure of my concern for all the churches.

Up to this point Paul has been describing external factors, things that came upon him from the outside in the course of his ministry. He had been confronted with the onslaught of nature. He had faced the enmity of Jew and Gentile alike. He had endured bone-wearying toil, and he knew what it meant to go hungry and without sufficient clothing. He had encountered those who pretended to be brothers in the faith but who were really false brothers bent on destroying the faith of Paul's converts.

Now Paul talks about something the "super-apostles" would hardly be able to understand since it was far removed from the spirit with which they were carrying out their ministry. He speaks of an internal factor, a factor that made him much more a servant of Christ than his adversaries. It was something he faced *daily* and which weighed heavily upon him. Paul describes it, in fact, as *pressure*.

What was this pressure? It was his *concern* for all the *churches*. The word translated "concern" is a strong term. In some places it means "worry." It was used by Jesus, for example, when he chided Martha for complaining that Mary wasn't helping her with dinner preparations. "Martha, Martha," Jesus had said, "you are *worried* and upset about many things" (Luke 10:41).

The emotion Paul is describing here is not sinful worry, which indicates a lack of trust, but a deep, heartfelt concern. It was with him 24 hours a day. And he experienced this concern for all the churches he had founded.

Paul gives an example of what he means by this concern in the verse that follows.

29Who is weak, and I do not feel weak? Who is led into sin, and I do not inwardly burn?

As a faithful pastor, Paul identified with his people in their struggles against sin. Empathy, it is sometimes called, feeling with people, putting oneself as much as possible into their shoes. Their weaknesses, whatever form they may take, Paul feels as his weaknesses. Their stumbling and falling into sin, as one commentator puts it, "causes him to burn with shame as though it were his own stumbling and to burn with indignation against the seducer who has made one of Christ's little ones to stumble" (Hughes, p. 418).

If there was any quality in Paul that made it possible for him to say, "Are [the 'super-apostles'] servants of Christ?. . . I am more" (11:23), it was this one. The "super-apostles" were bent on enslaving and exploiting the Corinthians. They were taking advantage of them, they were arrogantly pushing themselves forward for self-gain, they were using their authority to abuse the Corinthians. And Paul? Not concern for self, but concern for the Corinthians was the distinguishing mark of the way he was serving them.

Christians in positions of spiritual leadership today can see in Paul what it means to be a faithful minister of Christ. It means holding to and bringing to people the Jesus of the Bible without any additions or subtractions. It means labor, being willing to suffer inconvenience, to endure hardship, even to face danger, for the sake of bringing the gospel to others. And it means having a deep and abiding concern for the people among whom one is ministering. A faithful minister of Christ will always be asking, "How can I help people?", rather than, "How can people help me?"

Paul's Escape from Damascus

Paul has saved to the last an experience that certainly had not been duplicated by the "super-apostles." He will talk about this experience, a special vision granted to him by the Lord, at the beginning of chapter 12.

He is sensitive, however, to the fact that what he is going to say might be construed as sinful pride. He therefore prefaces his remarks in 12:1-6 with an account of what by the world's standards was a most humiliating experience. As far as Paul is concerned, though, he feels more comfortable reporting about events that put the spotlight on his weaknesses than on situations which might be misconstrued as boasting about his strengths.

³⁰If I must boast, I will boast of the things that show my weakness. ³¹The God and Father of the Lord Jesus, who is to be praised forever, knows that I am not lying.

To boast about one's weaknesses runs counter to the way the world operates. One accentuates his strengths, not his weaknesses. Paul, therefore, feels constrained to invoke the name of God to back up his assertion that he would much rather boast of his weaknesses than of any supposed strengths. God, *who is to be praised forever,* God, who is the *Father of the Lord Jesus,* knows that Paul is not lying.

He then gives a striking example of his weakness.

³²In Damascus the governor under King Aretas had the city of the Damascenes guarded in order to arrest me. ³³But I was lowered in a basket from a window in the wall and slipped through his hands.

Paul is referring here to an incident that is also mentioned in the book of Acts (9:23-25). It occurred about three years after his conversion. Shortly after his conversion Paul had left Damascus and traveled to Arabia, where he remained for three years. Then he returned to Damascus where he stayed for "many days" (cf. Galatians 1:17,18 and Acts 9:23).

Paul then learned that some of the unbelieving Jews in Damascus were plotting to take his life. As Paul indicates in these verses, they enlisted the help of the governor of Damascus to seize and arrest him. The governor, who held the title "ethnarch," served under Aretas IV, king of Nabatea, a territory east of Damascus.

Aretas ruled from 9 B.C. to 39 or 40 A.D. The region over which he ruled did not extend as far east as Damascus, which was a part of Syria and directly under Roman rule. There is some evidence, however, that during the last years of the reign of Aretas, 37 to 39 or 40 A.D., the territory over which he ruled did include Damascus.

Neither the Jews nor the governor were able to catch Paul, for he didn't leave Damascus via the closely-guarded gates. *I was lowered in a basket from a window in the wall,* Paul says, *and slipped through his hands.*

What a contrast as compared with his original visit to Damascus! At that time he was traveling from Jerusalem as the leader of an official entourage. He represented the top man, the high priest himself. He was intent on scouring the synagogues of Damascus and on bringing back as prisoners any who embraced the name of Jesus. He was a man of power, of influence, of authority.

Of that, though, Paul will not boast. He will instead boast of his humiliating exit from Damascus. He is lowered in a rope basket through an opening in the wall. Hardly anything to write home about! Since this was an illustration of his powerlessness, however, Paul finds it quite worthwhile to mention. He wants the Corinthians to know that whatever has been accomplished in his ministry has not been by his doing. He is the weak and fragile jar of clay. The all-surpassing power is from God (cf. 2:7). Faithful ministers of the gospel today also will be slow to speak of what they have done and plan to do and quick to speak of what God has done and can do in spite of the weak vessels through whom he works.

With the escape from Damascus as a lead-in, Paul now is ready to reveal a most glorious experience the Lord had granted to him.

Paul's Vision of Paradise

12 I must go on boasting. Although there is nothing to be gained, I will go on to visions and revelations from the

Lord. ²I know a man in Christ who fourteen years ago was caught up to the third heaven. Whether it was in the body or out of the body I do not know — God knows. ³And I know that this man — whether in the body or apart from the body I do not know, but God knows — ⁴was caught up to paradise. He heard inexpressible things, things that man is not permitted to tell.

Paul is continuing with his boasting, this time about *visions and revelations,* in particular a special vision the Lord had granted him at an earlier point in his ministry. It was an experience which up to this time he had almost certainly not disclosed to the Corinthians since he realized there was *nothing to be gained* by doing so. Paul knew that ministers of the gospel do not help their people by boasting about their own personal religious experiences. Faith is engendered and faith grows by proclaiming the word, not by parading experiences.

In these particular circumstances, however, Paul feels compelled to do a little boasting about his religious experiences. Although we are not specifically told so, the "super-apostles" apparently were using some supposed visions and revelations to back up their claim to spiritual authority. Paul, therefore, asserts that he too can speak of visions and revelations from the Lord.

In Bible times God often communicated with his people by means of visions and revelations. The book of Acts records several occasions on which Paul himself received a divine revelation. At the beginning of his second missionary journey, it was through a vision that Paul was directed to bring the gospel to Macedonia (cf. Acts 16:9,10). During Paul's stay in Corinth the Lord spoke to him in a vision, encouraging him to keep on proclaiming the gospel and promising him that no one would harm him (cf. Acts 18:9-11).

The vision Paul speaks of here, however, is not mentioned in the book of Acts or in any other letter of Paul. It was an intensely personal experience, which even now he hesitates to speak of. Note how he shies away from using the personal pronoun "I." Rather, he relates the incident in the third person, speaking simply of *a man in Christ,* that is, a Christian.

Fourteen years ago, says Paul, this man was *caught up to the third heaven.* This vision would have occurred prior to Paul's first missionary journey, during the time he was in Tarsus waiting for further direction from the Lord (cf. Galatians 1:21). Though he now feels compelled to tell the Corinthians of the vision, Paul is vague about the specifics. All he says is that he was *caught up to the third heaven.*

The word translated "caught up" is used also in 1 Thessalonians. There it describes what will happen to the believers who are still alive when Jesus returns. They will be "caught up . . . in the clouds to meet the Lord in the air" (1 Thessalonians 4:17). That reference clearly refers to a bodily ascent into heaven. When Paul thinks back to his experience of being caught up into the third heaven, he isn't sure whether it was a bodily, physical ascent or not. He says, *Whether it was in the body or out of the body I do not know — God knows.* How it happened did not matter. That it had occurred, however, is beyond doubt.

What is the *third heaven* to which Paul had been caught up? Paul is possibly using terminology used by the Jews of his day. Some of them spoke of a three-, others of a five- and others of a seven-layered heaven. At any rate, Paul defines what he means by the third heaven when he says that he *was caught up to paradise.* "Paradise" is the word used in the Septuagint, the Greek translation of the Old Testament, to describe the Garden of Eden. It is from a Persian word that means "park."

In the New Testament the word "paradise" is used two other times. To the thief on the cross Jesus said, "Today you will be with me in paradise" (Luke 23:43). In the book of Revelation we find this promise of Jesus: "To him who overcomes, I will give the right to eat from the tree of life, which is in the paradise of God" (Revelation 2:7). From these two references it appears clear that by the terms *third heaven* and *paradise* Paul is referring to the place where the beauty and perfection of what once was in Eden will be restored and never end, the place the Bible in most cases simply calls "heaven."

Not only had Paul seen an amazing sight, he had also heard some amazing sounds. So amazing were they, in fact, Paul says they were *inexpressible*. Besides that, says Paul, they were things *that man is not permitted to tell*. What Paul heard while he was given a revelation of paradise was impossible for him to repeat, and even if he could have done so, he had been instructed not to.

These words are a reminder that new and exciting experiences await the believer in heaven, sights and sounds that cannot be described in human language. St. John writes in his first epistle, "Dear friends, now we are children of God, and what we will be has not yet been made known. But we know that when he appears, we shall be like him, for we shall see him as he is" (1 John 3:2). Many great and wonderful surprises await children of God when on the last day they are caught up into heaven.

Paul had been given an advance glimpse of this glory awaiting him and all believers. Why the Lord had granted this vision to him Paul does not state. We can safely assume, however, that it was one way by which the Lord strengthened Paul for the years of missionary work that lay before him. In difficult days he could keep before his eyes the vision of the glory that one day would be his, as he writes to the Romans, "I consider that our present sufferings are not worth comparing with the glory that will be revealed in us" (Romans 8:18).

⁵I will boast about a man like that, but I will not boast about myself, except about my weaknesses.

In saying that he will boast about a *man like that,* Paul is continuing to use the third person in speaking of his vision of paradise. In fact, he speaks so indirectly about this "man in Christ," one might even be led to conclude that he is talking about another person. The verses that follow, however, verse 7 especially, make it clear that Paul is describing himself.

Though the Corinthians, in their obsession with externals, have forced Paul to boast about this experience, he emphasizes, *I will not boast about myself.* He wants them to know that by revealing this experience to them he is not saying, "Look how great I am." Let the "super-apostles" speak that way; Paul refuses to do so. He wants the Corinthians to see only the greatness of God. God's greatness is seen most clearly as he carries out his work through weak human beings. Paul, therefore, will not hesitate to boast about his *weaknesses* (cf. 2 Corinthians 11:30).

With these words Paul is turning from the subject of being caught up into paradise. He is ready to move on to something that occurred subsequent to that experience, something that magnified God's greatness through Paul's weakness. Before doing so, however, he wants to make it clear that he has been totally honest about everything of which he has been boasting.

⁶Even if I should choose to boast, I would not be a fool, because I would be speaking the truth. But I refrain, so no one will think more of me than is warranted by what I do or say.

Throughout the final chapters of 2 Corinthians, beginning with chapter ten, Paul has made it clear that he feels uneasy in boasting about himself — his ancestry, his labors, his experiences. The boasts of the "super-apostles," however, had thrust him into this uncomfortable role.

Though he may have felt foolish in his boasting, however, he can confidently say, *Even if I should choose to boast, I would not be a fool.* Why not? Because, he says, *I would be speaking the truth.* In these words there is likely the implication that the "super-apostles" were not speaking the truth. If Paul has to resort to boasting about his labors and experiences, at least what he says will not exceed the bounds of truth.

But I refrain, Paul says. He has come to the end of such boasting and is getting back to more comfortable ground: boasting about his weaknesses and God's power. Paul is moving in this direction, he says, *so no one will think more of me than is warranted by what I do or say.* Paul wants people to accept him and his message, not because of such phenomena as miraculous visions, but because of the power of the message alone.

Paul's Thorn in the Flesh

⁷To keep me from becoming conceited because of these surpassingly great revelations, there was given me a thorn in my flesh, a messenger of Satan, to torment me.

Paul has just said, "I will not boast about myself, except about my weaknesses." In these verses he gives a graphic example of one of his weaknesses. He calls it *a thorn in my flesh.*

What was Paul's thorn in the flesh? Bible commentators down through the ages have offered numerous suggestions. The majority lean toward the idea that it was some kind of chronic physical problem. Paul is possibly referring to this thorn in Galatians when he says, "As you know, it was because of an illness [literally, "a weakness of the flesh," or "bodily weakness"] that I first preached the gospel to you" (Galatians 4:13). That has led some to speculate that Paul's thorn was malaria, a reoccurrence of which had supposedly forced him to leave low-lying Perga quickly and move up to Antioch of Pisidia, which lay at a higher elevation (cf. Acts 13:13).

Others suppose it may have been a severe eye problem (cf. Galatians 4:15; 6:11). Still others speculate the thorn may have been a speech impediment of some sort, such as stammering, which Paul's opponents in Corinth would have contrasted with their skill in oratory.

The truth of the matter is that we don't know and won't know this side of heaven what Paul's thorn in the flesh was. We can infer from the word "thorn," however, that it was a sharp pain of some sort. We can also infer that it was a reoccurring, nagging pain. The Greek text brings out that Paul's thorn in the flesh was given to "keep on tormenting" him.

Though we do not know what this thorn in the flesh was, we do know both how it came and why it came. Paul says, *There was given me a thorn in my flesh.* The thorn was not an accident; it was given to Paul. The giver was God himself.

God had a loving purpose in afflicting Paul with this thorn in the flesh. The purpose, says Paul, was *to keep me from becoming conceited.* In the original text these words are repeated twice, "To keep me from becoming conceited there was given me a thorn in my flesh . . . to keep me from becoming conceited." The repetition is for the sake of emphasis. God had graciously granted Paul such revelations as his vision of paradise. Lest Paul become puffed up with pride because of these special revelations, the Lord had given him some kind of affliction which would constantly remind him that he was still a weak mortal, entirely dependent on the grace of God.

Paul calls this thorn given to him by God a *messenger of Satan.* Satan was an unwitting tool of God in this respect. Satan would have seen the thorn as an opportunity to bring evil upon a child of God, but God used the thorn to accomplish his good purpose of keeping Paul humble.

⁸Three times I pleaded with the Lord to take it away from me.

These words indicate that Paul did not immediately recognize the purpose of his thorn in the flesh, just as Christians today cannot always understand why God permits certain problems to plague them. To him the thorn, whatever it may have been, was hindering rather than helping his ministry.

He therefore asked the Lord to take it away from him. Paul's prayers about his thorn are reminiscent of Jesus' prayer in the garden of Gethsemane in that both asked three times. He was persistent in his prayer, just as his Savior had been. Believers today also are encouraged to call upon their Lord in the day of trouble. The Lord promises to deliver us (cf. Psalm 50:15).

The Lord's deliverance, however, does not always take the form we might expect. So it was with Paul and his thorn.

9But he said to me, "My grace is sufficient for you, for my power is made perfect in weakness." Therefore I will boast all the more gladly about my weaknesses, so that Christ's power may rest on me.

God answers prayer. He answers in his own time. Both Jesus in Gethsemane and Paul prayed three times before receiving an answer.

And God answers in his own way. Jesus had prayed for his cup of suffering to be removed. His Father's answer was not to remove the cup but to send angels to strengthen him to drink it. Paul had prayed for his thorn in the flesh to be removed. The Lord's answer was not to remove the thorn but to assure him that his strengthening grace would enable him to cope with it.

We can carry the comparison between Jesus in Gethsemane and Paul one step further. The Lord brought positive good out of both situations. By drinking the cup Jesus paid the ransom price of death to win forgiveness for the world. By continuing to suffer with his thorn, Paul kept the spotlight shining on Jesus rather than himself. *My power,* the Lord had said to him, *is made perfect in weakness.* As people looked at and listened to the weak, frail, thorn-in-the-flesh-beset Paul, they would be led to conclude: There must be a greater power behind this man to enable him to do all the things he is doing. That power, of course, was the Lord, the Savior.

Paul's real prayer, then, that nothing get in the way of his ministry, was answered. The thorn was not a hindrance, as he had supposed, but a help. Therefore, he says, *I will boast all the more gladly about my weaknesses, so that Christ's power may rest on me.*

Anything, in fact, that magnified the grace and power of God was a cause for rejoicing on Paul's part, no matter how painful it may have been.

¹⁰That is why, for Christ's sake, I delight in weaknesses, in insults, in hardships, in persecutions, in difficulties. For when I am weak, then I am strong.

With these words Paul is turning the table on his opponents. They had pointed to his weaknesses as evidence that he could hardly be a genuine apostle. Paul, on the other hand, says, *When I am weak, then I am strong.* This is another way of saying what Paul had already stated in this letter: "We have this treasure in jars of clay to show that this all-surpassing power is from God and not from us" (4:7).

We are dealing with a paradox here. The world says, "Only when I am strong, only when I have status, power, influence, wealth, only then I am strong." The Christian says, "Only when I am weak, only when I realize that the world's symbols of strength mean nothing even if I have them all, only then am I strong." Thank God for thorns, whatever form they may take, for they remind us that we are weak. And when we know we are weak, then we can be strong — in Christ. Those who find their strength *in* Christ can then, with Paul, be strong *for* Christ.

Paul's Demonstration of All the Signs of an Apostle

¹¹I have made a fool of myself, but you drove me to it. I ought to have been commended by you, for I am not in the least inferior to the "super-apostles," even though I am nothing.

When Paul says, *I have made a fool of myself,* he uses a tense of the Greek verb that has in it the idea of something that was true in the past and still is. We might paraphrase it, "I have become a fool by writing in this way and stand before you as a fool as you read what I have written." He is referring, of course, to all the boasting he has found it necessary to do in the closing chapters of this letter.

It was not his choice to do this. The Corinthians *drove,* or compelled, Paul to this boasting that was so foreign to him. It would have been entirely unnecessary if the Corinthians had not been so gullible. They had listened with admiration to Paul's detractors when they should have been speaking up on Paul's behalf. *I ought to have been commended by you,* Paul tells them. The Corinthians could have told the "super-apostles" about Paul's tireless and unselfish labors on their behalf. They could have made it clear that they owed their spiritual life to the message Paul had brought to them.

Christians today also are urged to "speak up for those who cannot speak for themselves" (Proverbs 31:8). Martin Luther says it nicely in his explanation to the Eighth Commandment. If our neighbor is being maligned, we should "defend him, speak well of him and take his words and actions in the kindest possible way."

If the Corinthians had spoken up for Paul, he would not have been compelled to come to his own defense, as he does with the statement, *I am not in the least inferior to the "super-apostles," even though I am nothing.* Had the "super-apostles" perhaps inferred that Paul was a "Nothing," a "Nobody"? That was hardly a badge of dishonor for Paul. As a "Nothing," a weak, fragile jar of clay, Christ himself had worked through him. That made him far superior to the "super-apostles," whose strength lay in themselves and not in Christ.

Paul points to evidence that Christ had been powerfully at work in his ministry among the Corinthians:

12The things that mark an apostle — signs, wonders and miracles — were done among you with great perseverance.

During his ministry Jesus commissioned the Twelve "to preach the kingdom of God." He also "gave them power and authority to drive out all demons and to cure diseases" (cf. Luke 9:1,2). After his resurrection Jesus repeated this commission to his apostles and assured them that miraculous signs would accompany their preaching of the gospel (cf. Mark 16:14-20).

Paul asserts that when he was in Corinth he had displayed the marks of an apostle. He had preached the gospel, and his preaching had been accompanied by *signs, wonders, and miracles*. Each of these three terms is speaking of the same thing, powerful deeds that defy the laws of nature, but viewing them from different angles. As *signs* they confirmed, or authenticated, the doer as someone sent from God. The term *wonders* alludes to the awe and amazement which the performance of a miracle elicits. The word *miracles*, literally "powers," points to the supernatural power that lies behind any act that exceeds the ordinary laws of nature.

Paul reminds the Corinthians that such signs, wonders, and miracles had been a part of his ministry in Corinth. Acts 18, Luke's account of Paul's eighteen-month stay in Corinth, does not mention any miracles, but obviously they had been performed or Paul would not have mentioned the fact here. Writing to the Romans, Paul describes his ministry in terms of "what Christ has accomplished through me in leading the Gentiles to obey God by what I have said and done — by the power of signs and miracles, through the power of the Spirit. So from Jerusalem all the way around to Illyricum, I have fully proclaimed the gospel of Christ" (Romans 15:18-19).

Preaching the gospel accompanied by signs, wonders, and miracles — which was the mark of an apostle — this was the way Paul had carried on his ministry, also in Corinth. He

231

adds that he had done this *in great perseverance.* He had kept at it, even in the face of hardship and opposition.

Paul had treated the Corinthians the same way he had treated all of the people among whom he had worked. He had not deprived them in any way — except one:

¹³How were you inferior to the other churches, except that I was never a burden to you? Forgive me this wrong!

Paul had not been a financial burden to the Corinthians. He had not taken any money from them. He had already touched on this subject in the previous chapter (cf. 11:7-11). His opponents had evidently been contending that Paul loved others, such as the Macedonians, more because he permitted them to support his ministry financially.

He had already responded to this charge and demonstrated how improper it was. He brings it up once again to display how fully and faithfully he has performed his apostolic ministry in their midst. The only "flaw" in his ministry has been his refusal to be a burden to the Corinthians. His *Forgive me this wrong* is thus strongly ironical. It had been, of course, not a wrong at all, but an act of love on Paul's part.

With these words Paul is finished with his boasting. He is now ready to turn his attention to his coming third visit to Corinth and how the Corinthians should prepare themselves for that visit.

PAUL'S COMING THIRD VISIT TO CORINTH
(12:14-13:10)

Paul's Readiness to Give His All

¹⁴Now I am ready to visit you for the third time, and I will not be a burden to you, because what I want is not your possessions but you. After all, children should not have to save up for their parents, but parents for their children. ¹⁵So I will very gladly spend for you everything I have and expend myself as well. If I love you more, will you love me less?

In the final four chapters of 2 Corinthians Paul is thinking about his coming visit to Corinth (cf. 10:2; 12:20,21; 13:1,10). This will be the *third time* Paul has visited Corinth. His first visit is recorded in Acts 18:1-8. He had come to Corinth on his second missionary journey, established a congregation, and remained there for a year-and-a-half.

His second visit to Corinth is not mentioned in Acts. Paul is undoubtedly referring to it in 2 Corinthians 2 where he speaks of a "painful visit" (verse 1). This visit would have transpired during Paul's third missionary journey while Paul was across the Aegean Sea in Ephesus. Following this visit, Paul had written two letters to the church at Corinth, only one of which has survived, the letter we call 1 Corinthians (cf. the comments under 2 Corinthians 2:1-4).

Now Paul is ready for a third visit to Corinth. He assures the Corinthians, *I will not be a burden to you.* When he had been in Corinth previously, he had not burdened the Corinthians by drawing any of his financial support from them (cf. 2 Corinthians 11:9). The policy he followed on his third visit would be no different.

He has good reason for proceeding in this fashion: *What I want is not your possessions but you.* In his first letter Paul had counselled the Corinthians, "Nobody should seek his own good, but the good of others" (1 Corinthians 10:24). Here he is following his own wise counsel. He doesn't seek monetary gain at the expense of the Corinthians. He seeks the Corinthians themselves.

What does Paul mean when he states that he seeks, or wants, the Corinthians? He was more concerned about the total person than about what came from that person. Jesus said, "Make a tree good and its fruit will be good" (Matthew 12:33). That is Paul's concern. He wants the Corinthians themselves to be and to remain in a right relationship with God through a humble trust in Jesus. That is of primary importance. If the tree is good, if the Corinthians continue to be numbered among those whom God declares to be good, holy, and righteous in his eyes through faith in Jesus who was good, holy, and righteous in their place, then the fruit will take care of itself. Good trees produce good fruit.

With Paul, Christian leaders today will do well to concern themselves first with making the tree good. That is achieved by careful, ongoing use of law and gospel through which the Holy Spirit strikes down the old, sinful flesh and energizes the new man whose desire is to walk with God in every way. Fruits of faith are not produced by telling people what *they* ought to be doing for God. They are generated by telling people the good news of what *God* has done for them in Christ.

In refusing to burden the Corinthians with his financial needs, Paul says he is treating them the way a father treats his children. In 1 Corinthians Paul had reminded the believers in Corinth, "I became your father through the gospel" (1 Corinthians 4:15). It is not the responsibility of children *to save up for their parents,* he says, *but parents for their children.* Parents don't look for what they can get out of their children, but for what they can give to them.

So it was with Paul and his spiritual children in Corinth. He tells them, *I will gladly spend for you everything I have and expend myself as well.* He is interested in only one thing: the spiritual well-being of his spiritual children. What a beautiful description of the kind of pastoral care that should be the mark of all spiritual shepherds! They will want to pattern themselves after *the* Shepherd, who says of himself, "I lay down my life for the sheep" (John 10:15). To a good shepherd nothing is more important than the welfare of the flock. He will be ready to give his all for the sheep entrusted to his care.

Sad to say, Paul's love for the Corinthians was being misconstrued by some of the Corinthians, causing Paul to ask, *If I love you more, will you love me less?* Paul is still on the subject of his refusal to receive any financial support from the Corinthians. His opponents, the "super-apostles," evidently had distorted Paul's purpose for doing this.

The "super-apostles" had apparently been telling the Corinthians, "Paul doesn't think as highly of you as he does of the Macedonians. He has welcomed them as his mission partners, gladly accepting their financial support. The fact that Paul does not want to have anything to do with your money indicates that you stand lower in his estimation than the Macedonians."

To that accusation Paul had responded that it was because he loved the Corinthians, because he sought their spiritual welfare above all, that he had not accepted their financial support (cf. 2 Corinthians 11:10,11). As their spiritual father,

Paul knew what was best for the Corinthians and would not deviate from that course, even if it meant he would be loved less by them. A parent's primary question is not, "Will my children like me if I do this?" Rather the key question is, "Will I be giving my children what they need, even if in the process they might not be happy with me for a time?"

Similarly, a faithful minister of the gospel will not determine the direction of his ministry by asking, "How will my people feel about me if I proceed in this fashion?" He will ask instead, "What will spiritually benefit the flock the Spirit has placed into my care, regardless of personal consequences?" He will be more concerned about showing love than about being loved.

This does not mean, of course, that a pastor will be insensitive to people's feelings. He will seek to be tactful. He will speak the truth in love (cf. Ephesians 4:15). But he will speak the truth, even if it might rob him of personal popularity.

16Be that as it may, I have not been a burden to you. Yet, crafty fellow that I am, I caught you by trickery!

Once again, Paul is apparently alluding to a charge of his enemies. Paul had *not been a burden* to the Corinthians. He had refused to take any money from them. This the Corinthians could not deny.

That could well have made the "super-apostles" look greedy by comparison. They therefore strike back by telling the Corinthians, "Don't be deceived by this apparent generosity of Paul. He says he doesn't want to be a burden to you. There is more to it than that. You should know that this Paul is a *crafty fellow.* He has something up his sleeve he is not telling you about."

What is the *trickery* Paul is being charged with? Paul does not expressly tell us. The next few verses, however, give us a little hint.

[17]Did I exploit you through any of the men I sent you? [18]I urged Titus to go to you and I sent our brother with him. Titus did not exploit you, did he? Did we not act in the same spirit and follow the same course?

We must remain somewhat tentative here since Paul does not fill in all the details for us. It is not unreasonable to suppose, however, that the charge of the "super-apostles" against Paul had something to do with the offering for the poor believers in Jerusalem which Paul was gathering with the help of some of his co-workers. It appears that Paul's enemies were accusing him of planning to use at least some of this offering to line his own pockets and of involving his co-workers in this scheme.

To counter that accusation Paul points to the behavior of those whom he had sent to Corinth. He asks four questions, which the NIV translation has reduced to three. The first two questions are worded in such a way that they expect a "No" answer; the final two expect the answer "Yes."

Paul asks, *Did I exploit you through any of the men I sent you?* Had Paul taken advantage of the Corinthians in any way through any of the men whom he had sent to them? Had they in any way acted in a devious or underhanded manner? The Corinthians would have to answer, "No."

Then Paul becomes more specific. He names one of these men, Titus, and mentions another, simply calling him *our brother*. This is possibly a reference to the "brother" mentioned in 8:22, whom Paul had sent along with Titus to Corinth to help gather in the offering. Chapter 8 mentions yet another "brother" (verse 18) who had accompanied Titus to Corinth. This man, however, had been chosen directly by the churches, while the "brother" of 8:22 appears to have been selected personally by Paul to accompany Titus.

Paul asks the Corinthians, *Titus did not exploit you, did he?* Again, the Corinthians could only answer, "No." They knew that Titus had been honest in his dealings with them. He had not taken advantage of them in any way.

Paul then concludes with the two questions that require a positive answer: *Did we not act in the same spirit? [Did we not] follow the same course?* If the Corinthians would look at things as they really were and not as they were being distorted by the "super-apostles," they could only conclude, "Everything we have seen and heard in you, Paul, and everything we have seen and heard in your associates has been open and above board. We have no reason to doubt your motives or your actions. Everything you have done has truly been for our benefit."

Paul's Fears about the Unrepentant

19Have you been thinking all along that we have been defending ourselves to you? We have been speaking in the sight of God as those in Christ; and everything we do, dear friends, is for your strengthening.

Anytime that a person goes to the lengths to defend himself as Paul has done in this letter he risks being misunderstood. Yes, he has been defending himself, but there is more to it than that. Paul wants the Corinthians to understand that his concern has not been his personal vindication. We are speaking to you Corinthians, he says, *in the sight of God as those in Christ.* In 2:17 Paul had used a similar expression in comparing his ministry with that of those who "peddle the word of God for profit." He was always acutely aware of the fact that, as one called directly by Christ, he was responsible to his Lord for the way he conducted his ministry. The one whose approval counted, therefore, was his Lord.

Paul was not defending himself, then, to gain the Corinthians' approval. He did not need that. His defense was not for his benefit at all, in fact. He tells them, *Everything we do, dear friends, is for your strengthening.* Above all Paul wanted the Corinthians to continue in and be built up in the faith. Saving faith is preserved and grows by the power of the Holy Spirit working through the gospel. Paul was a messenger of the gospel. If Paul lost his credibility, that would jeopardize the credibility of the gospel which came from his lips.

Therein lay the reason for Paul's vigorous defense of his ministry. He loved the Corinthians. He calls them *dear friends,* literally, "beloved." As his dearly loved spiritual children, nothing should come between them and the gospel, which was their one hope for life now and life forever.

There was a danger of that occurring, as Paul brings out in the next few verses.

20For I am afraid that when I come I may not find you as I want you to be, and you may not find me as you want me to be. I fear that there may be quarreling, jealousy, outbursts of anger, factions, slander, gossip, arrogance and disorder. 21I am afraid that when I come again my God will humble me before you, and I will be grieved over many who have sinned earlier and have not repented of the impurity, sexual sin and debauchery in which they have indulged.

With these words Paul is not implying that everything in Corinth was in disarray. Earlier in the letter Paul had spoken of the favorable report Titus had given him about the situation in Corinth. As a result of this report Paul could state in a most positive manner, "I am glad I can have complete confidence in you" (2 Corinthians 7:16).

These verses reveal, however, that there were still problems in Corinth. *When I come,* Paul tells them, *I may not find you as I want you to be.* And conversely, he says about the Corinthians, *You may not find me as you want me to be.* At the beginning of the final section of 2 Corinthians Paul had written, "I beg you that when I come I may not have to be as bold as I expect to be toward some people who think that we live by the standards of this world. . . . We will be ready to punish every act of disobedience" (2 Corinthians 10:2,6). He knew that he would have to come with a big stick against his opponents.

In the verses before us he expresses the fear that he might have to deal in the same manner with some of the members of the Corinthian congregation. That was not the way they would want Paul to come, and it is not the way Paul would want to come either.

Most of the sins Paul lists in these verses are the kinds of sins he had spoken out against in 1 Corinthians. He heads his list with *quarreling* and *jealousy,* words which he had used in connection with the way the Corinthians had separated themselves into little cliques (cf. 1:11 and 3:3). He had admonished them about *disorder* in their worship services (chapters 12-14) and also about a spirit of *arrogance* (cf. 4:18; 5:6). *Impurity, sexual sin, and debauchery* were prevalent in Corinth and were sins Paul had warned against previously (cf. 5:1-5; 6:18-20).

Through the message of law and gospel the Corinthian congregation had been experiencing growth in sanctification in all of these areas. The Spirit had worked through Paul's message. The results were visible. The fruit of the Spirit was replacing the works of the flesh.

This was not true of all of them, however. Paul is afraid he might encounter *many who have sinned earlier and have not repented.* As a result, he says, *my God will humble me before you, and I will be grieved.* It didn't bother Paul if God humbled him. "When I am weak," he had told the Corinthians, "then I am strong" (2 Corinthians 12:10). That is not his point.

His point is that what might be personally good for him will be bad for the portion of the Corinthian congregation which has persisted in sin and not repented. Paul envisions this scenario: He arrives in Corinth with much enthusiasm and optimism, buoyed up by the encouraging report of Titus (cf. 2 Corinthians 7:5-16). He is confident, perhaps overly-confident, that Corinth's many problems have been overcome. Then God humbles him. A sizeable number have persisted in their earlier sins and have not repented. Paul's work isn't finished, as he may have thought that it was.

While such a moment of humbling may have been a spiritual blessing to Paul, it would not have been good news to the impenitent Corinthians. Paul would have to come to them with the heavy hand of the law rather than the uplifting hand of the gospel. If that is the way he will have to come, he *will be grieved,* just as his Savior was grieved and wept over the impenitent people of Jerusalem when he spoke of the heavy arm of the wrath of God coming upon them (cf. Matthew 23:37-39).

God may humble ministers of the gospel today in ways much like Paul describes here. For example, a pastor may work hard and long to bring the gospel to the people of his community. He knocks on countless doors. He visits in hundreds of homes to share the message of law and gospel. And yet the pastor may see very few visible results.

The pastor, of course, will not thank the Lord that many apparently have rejected the gospel. He will grieve over that, just as Paul grieved over the specter of facing impenitent members of the Corinthian congregation.

He will thank the Lord, however, that through this humbling experience he has been reminded that results are the Lord's business. Planting and watering the seed is what the Lord's servant has been called to do. The growth of that seed rests in the hands of the one who has called him to serve.

Paul's Call to Repentance

13 **This will be my third visit to you. "Every matter must be established by the testimony of two or three witnesses." ²I already gave you a warning when I was with you the second time. I now repeat it while absent: On my return I will not spare those who sinned earlier or any of the others, ³since you are demanding proof that Christ is speaking through me.**

Once again Paul reminds the Corinthians that he will be with them shortly and that this will be the third time he has been in Corinth (cf. 2 Corinthians 12:14). He then quotes Deuteronomy 19:15, *Every matter must be established by the testimony of two or three witnesses*. This passage is quoted or alluded to several times in the New Testament. The most well-known instance is in Matthew 18, where Jesus gives instructions on how to discipline a fellow Christian who has fallen into sin. If the sinner refuses to listen to the admonition of one person, that individual should "take one or two others along, so that 'every matter may be established by the testimony of two or three witnesses' " (Matthew 18:16). Jesus' instructions in Matthew 18 emphasize the lengths to which Christians will want to go to reclaim a straying sinner. They will not be hasty and arbitrary in labelling someone a "pagan" (Matthew 18:17).

As he writes to the Corinthians, Paul is using these words from Deuteronomy to underscore that same point. He is going to great lengths to bring the Corinthians to repentance. He says, *I already gave you a warning when I was with you the second time.* Paul had also written them two letters which contained much reproof (cf. the comments under 2 Corinthians 2:1-4). He warns them one more time in this letter: *On my return I will not spare those who sinned earlier or any of the others.*

The Corinthians, therefore, could not charge Paul with failing to give them sufficient opportunities to repent. He had gone the extra mile with them.

With whom? Paul mentions two groups. He first mentions *those who sinned earlier.* This is probably a reference to the ones described at the end of chapter 12 (verses 20-21), those whom Paul had begun to deal with in his second visit but who were still persisting in their sin.

The second group, which the Greek text simply describes as "all the rest" (NIV: "any of the others"), would include those who had fallen into sin subsequent to that time, perhaps as a result of the false ministry of the "super-apostles."

Paul asserts that he will not spare any who defiantly persist in their sin despite patient and prolonged admonition. As spiritual leaders in Christian congregations today deal with those who are persisting in sin and refusing to repent, they will see in Paul a worthy model to emulate. They will want to be no less patient than Paul. On the other hand, they will want to be no less firm.

Having made it clear that he will not spare those who spurn his call to repentance, Paul mentions to the Corinthians a personal reason for this course of action. He will not spare them *since you are demanding proof that Christ is speaking through me.* With these words Paul is returning to the accusation of his opponents that he was "bold" only when he wrote letters but "timid," cowardly, when face to face with the Corinthians (cf. 2 Corinthians 10:1). "In person," they were charging, "he is unimpressive and his speaking amounts to nothing" (2 Corinthians 10:10).

The "super-apostles" looked upon this as weakness when, in truth, it was Paul's love for souls which made him refrain from coming down quickly with the full weight of the law upon erring Christians. The "super-apostles" contended that a real apostle would have projected a much stronger image.

"When I come to Corinth this time," Paul says, "that false charge will fall to the wayside. Even judging me by the standards of the 'super-apostles,' you will have *proof that Christ is speaking through me*." As he had told them in a previous chapter, with this visit he "would be ready to punish every act of disobedience" (2 Corinthians 10:6).

Paul goes on to show that it should not surprise the Corinthians that he appeared to be both weak and powerful in his ministry. In that, he was no different from the one who had sent him.

He [Christ] is not weak in dealing with you, but is powerful among you. ⁴For to be sure, he was crucified in weakness, yet he lives by God's power. Likewise, we are weak in him, yet by God's power we will live with him to serve you.

Christ, Paul asserts, was not *weak* in his dealings with the Corinthians, but was *powerful* among them. Many of the Corinthians had been heathen. In Christ, through the gospel Paul had preached, a powerful miracle had occurred. They were no longer numbered among the sexually immoral, idolaters, adulterers, prostitutes, homosexuals, thieves, greedy, drunkards, slanderers, and swindlers who would not "inherit the kingdom of God" (cf. 2 Corinthians 6:9,10). They had become brand new people.

Paul wants the Corinthians to remember that the same Christ who had been so powerfully at work among them also had been weak. *He was crucified in weakness,* Paul reminds them. "He had no beauty or majesty to attract us to him," Isaiah had prophesied, "nothing in his appearance that we should desire him. He was despised and rejected by men, a man of sorrows, and familiar with suffering" (Isaiah 53:2,3). He had even gone so far as to willingly humble himself to a shameful death on a cross (cf. Philippians 2:8).

Yet, says Paul of that same Christ, *he lives by God's power.* The Christ who had permitted himself to become weak, even to death on a cross, was raised to life and now sits in power at God's right hand. "God exalted him to the highest place," Paul tells the Philippians, "and gave him the name that is above every name, that at the name of Jesus every knee should bow . . . and every tongue confess that Jesus Christ is Lord" (Philippians 2:9-11).

Paul's ministry, too, was marked by both weakness and power. On the one hand, Paul says, *We are weak in him.* Earlier in the letter he had described himself in terms of a weak, fragile jar of clay (cf. 2 Corinthians 4:7). Just as Christ had "made himself nothing" (Philippians 2:7), so Paul was carrying out his ministry in all humility. He had come to Corinth in the spirit of the one who had sent him: not to be served but to serve.

The Corinthians should not be deceived, however, by the weakness of Paul. They should not equate his weakness with worthlessness, his humility with incompetence. Just as the Christ who *was crucified in weakness* now *lives by God's power,* so, Paul tells the Corinthians, *By God's power we will live with him [Christ] to serve you.* There was more to that weak jar of clay than first met the eye. Paul, too, lives by God's power. And, what is most important for the Corinthians, he lives his life, a life intimately bound up with Christ, for their benefit — *to serve you,* he says.

Whatever Paul did — whether through his letters or his personal visits, whether it was a gentle word of encouragement for the weak or a powerful word of warning for the impenitent — was all intended for the spiritual well-being of the Corinthians. The risen, exalted Christ truly was speaking in every aspect of Paul's ministry. For proof of that, the Corinthians had to look no further than themselves. Paul encourages them to do just that in the verses that follow.

Paul's Call to Self-Examination

[5]Examine yourselves to see whether you are in the faith; test yourselves. Do you not realize that Christ Jesus is in you—unless, of course, you fail the test? [6]And I trust that you will discover that we have not failed the test.

Paul's point is simple: "If you Corinthians are looking for proof that I am a genuine apostle, that Christ is speaking through me, the best thing you can do is to be examining yourselves." They should be asking themselves: "Do we believe in Jesus? Is Christ living in us?"

If the Corinthians answer these questions in the affirmative — and Paul is sure they will—then they should ask themselves how this transformation had come about. Had it not occurred as a result of the ministry of Paul which had centered on the message of Jesus Christ and him crucified (cf. 1 Corinthians 2:2)?

If the Corinthians do not *fail the test,* if their self-examination reveals that they are *in the faith,* this means that Paul has not *failed the test* either. The Corinthians should look no further than to their own changed lives for proof of the genuine nature of Paul's ministry. It was just as Paul had written earlier in this letter: each believer in Corinth was "a letter from Christ, the result of our ministry" (2 Corinthians 3:3)

Paul expands somewhat on this thought in the verses that follow. He does this to guard against the faulty conclusion some might come to: that his major concern is to defend his own honor and integrity.

⁷Now we pray to God that you will not do anything wrong. Not that people will see that we have stood the test but that you will do what is right even though we may seem to have failed.

Paul's primary concern is not Paul and his reputation among the Corinthians; his concern above all is the Corinthians and their relationship with God. His prayer is that they *will not do anything wrong.* His fervent desire is that those who have been persisting in sins of any kind will repent. He wants them to *do what is right.* If the Corinthians do repent, Paul will not have to come to them as a stern preacher of the law. He will be able to come in gentleness with the soothing gospel of forgiveness.

His opponents might capitalize on this. They might tell the Corinthians, "This Paul who comes to you in such a quiet, unassuming way is hardly the picture of a real apostle. A genuine apostle would come with a much greater show of power and authority." Thus Paul in the eyes of some might *seem to have failed* to pass the test of an apostle. "That doesn't bother me," says Paul. "What counts is not that we stand approved before you, but that you stand approved before God."

⁸For we cannot do anything against the truth, but only for the truth. ⁹We are glad whenever we are weak but you are strong; and our prayer is for your perfection.

247

Paul's responsibility as an apostle was to be a herald of the truth. This meant, as he later wrote to Timothy, that he needed to "correctly handle the word of truth" (2 Timothy 2:15). His call was to apply law and gospel as the circumstances warranted, no matter how that might affect his personal reputation. He could not do anything against the truth, only for it.

If the Corinthians did not repent, then Paul would have to come with the law and deal severely with them. If, however, the Corinthians did repent, which was Paul's fervent prayer, then he would come with the gospel. By so doing his enemies might charge him with being *weak*. Paul says that he will be *glad* to accept that label, for his being able to come in "weakness" rather than with the stern, powerful message of the law would mean that the Corinthians themselves had repented and thus had once again become *strong*.

Paul wanted just one thing. He tells the Corinthians, *Our prayer is for your perfection*. The word translated *perfection* could perhaps be better rendered "restoration." It is the word that was used for mending torn nets (cf. Mark 1:19). It was also used for restoring an erring Christian to the right path (cf. Galatians 6:1). It thus has in it the idea of getting something back to the way it should be. That was Paul's aim and prayer for the Corinthians who had allowed themselves to stray from the right path. As he worked for their restoration, what they might think of him was not his paramount concern.

Paul is a beautiful model for spiritual leaders of all time. His single-minded devotion to the spiritual well-being of the flock regardless of personal consequences is exceeded only oy the one who selflessly gave himself as a sacrifice on Calvary. The love of that Jesus was clearly a compelling, guiding force in Paul's ministry as it is in the ministry of Christ's true shepherds today.

10This is why I write these things when I am absent, that when I come I may not have to be harsh in my use of authority — the authority the Lord gave me for building you up, not for tearing you down.

This is Paul's final word on a subject that has been a major theme throughout 2 Corinthians. Already in the first chapter Paul had written, "It was in order to spare you that I did not return to Corinth" (verse 23). Chapters 10-13 especially, which focus on Paul's coming visit to Corinth, zero in on this subject. Paul began chapter 10 with the appeal, "By the meekness and gentleness of Christ, I appeal to you . . . that when I come I may not have to be as bold as I expect to be toward some people who think that we live by the standards of this world" (verses 1-2).

One more time Paul asserts that he doesn't want to come in all severity, even though he has the authority to do so. He prays that this letter, with its call to repentance, will do the job he doesn't want to have to do when he gets there.

Then he states once again (compare 10:8) the ultimate purpose for his apostolic authority. "The Lord gave me this authority," he says, *for building you up, not for tearing you down.* The "super-apostles" were using their "authority" to tear down; Paul's purpose always was to build up. Even if he had to come with the law, it still would be meant to build them up. The law would serve the purpose of exposing their sin and God's condemnation so that they would be ready to receive the life-giving promises of the gospel. A true gospel ministry always has as its goal a building up of God's people.

Final Greetings

11Finally, brothers, good-bye. Aim for perfection, listen to my appeal, be of one mind, live in peace. And the God of love and peace will be with you.

Notice that Paul calls the Corinthians *brothers*. This has been his approach all the way through this letter. He has been addressing the Corinthians as Christian brothers. As weak as some of them were, nevertheless, they were a part of the family of God.

As he bids farewell to them, he makes four brief appeals. *Aim for perfection,* he tells them. He uses here the same word he employed in verse 9, where he had told them, "Our prayer is for your perfection," or, restoration. Now, to translate this phrase a little more literally, he says, "Be restored." The emphasis in the original Greek is not on what the Corinthians should do for themselves, but on what Paul prays will be continually done for them by God.

The same is true of the next phrase, *Listen to my appeal.* Literally translated, Paul is saying, "Be admonished." Again, his prayer is that his words of admonition will not have fallen on deaf ears.

With the requests, *Be of one mind,* and *Live in peace* Paul is addressing an ongoing problem in the Corinthian congregation: the tendency to splinter into various factions instead of holding together in a loving unity around the gospel (cf. 1 Corinthians 1:10ff). The arrival of the "super-apostles" threatened to produce yet another division: those who sided with Paul and those who aligned themselves with the "super-apostles." Only a common faith, firmly rooted in the gospel, will enable the Corinthians to keep on being of one mind and living at peace with one another.

Such a unity is a gift of God, as Paul brings out with the statement, *And the God of love and peace will be with you.* It is God who produces genuine love for one another within the Body of Christ; it is God who enables Christians to live in peace with each other. As the Corinthians received and took to heart the word of God as conveyed through the pen and lips of Paul, God himself would effect a true unity of believers around the truth.

¹²Greet one another with a holy kiss. ¹³All the saints send their greetings.

Paul had written virtually the same thing at the conclusion of 1 Corinthians (cf. 1 Corinthians 16:20). The words served as a reminder to the Corinthians of the Christian fellowship they enjoyed with each other at Corinth and also of the wider fellowship of believers. As Paul writes from Macedonia, he sends the greetings of all the brothers and sisters in the congregations in that area. The Corinthians do not stand alone.

Nor do Christians stand alone today, however isolated they may be. Luther once put it this way: "Although they may be a thousand miles apart in body, they are yet an assembly in spirit because each one preaches, believes, hopes, loves, and lives like the other." Christians confess to that truth each time they say, "I believe in the holy Christian church, the communion of saints."

¹⁴May the grace of the Lord Jesus Christ, and the love of God, and the fellowship of the Holy Spirit be with you all.

Paul closes all of his letters with a benediction. This is the only letter, however, in which Paul mentions all three persons of the Trinity in his parting words. He summarizes with one word the work of each person of the Trinity on our behalf.

The word he uses to summarize the work of Jesus is *grace*. Earlier in this letter Paul had described the grace of Jesus in this way: "Though he was rich, yet for your sakes he became poor, so that you through his poverty might become rich" (2 Corinthians 8:9).

When Paul thinks of God the Father, the word *love* comes to mind. Several months after the writing of 2 Corinthians, Paul would describe the love of God in this way in his letter to the Romans: "God demonstrates his own love for us in this: While we were still sinners, Christ died for us" (Romans 5:8).

The word Paul uses to summarize the work of the Holy Spirit is *fellowship*. The Spirit is the one who brings us into fellowship with Jesus (cf. 1 Corinthians 12:3) and through that into fellowship with one another.

It is fitting that Paul should close this letter with a mention of the fellowship worked by the Holy Spirit. It was the Spirit working through the gospel who had brought the Corinthians out of heathenism and formed them into a Christian fellowship. And it was the Spirit alone who could maintain that fellowship.

By way of a postscript, we might ask a number of questions: What did Paul find when he arrived in Corinth? Had his letter produced its desired effect? What became of the "super-apostles"? Did they repent? Did their followers see the error of their ways?

None of these questions are answered directly in the Scriptures. We do know, however, that Paul spent three months in Corinth subsequent to the writing of 2 Corinthians (cf. Acts 20:3). The epistle to the Romans was written from Corinth during Paul's stay there. In that letter Paul tells the Christians at Rome that he is ready to travel further west, all the way to Spain, in fact (cf. Romans 15:23-29). It appears from this that there must have been a favorable resolution of the problems in Corinth, for Paul now feels free to move elsewhere.

The writer of the letter to the Hebrews assures us that "the word of God is living and active" (Hebrews 4:12). Paul could trust that God would accomplish his gracious purposes through the word. So can we.

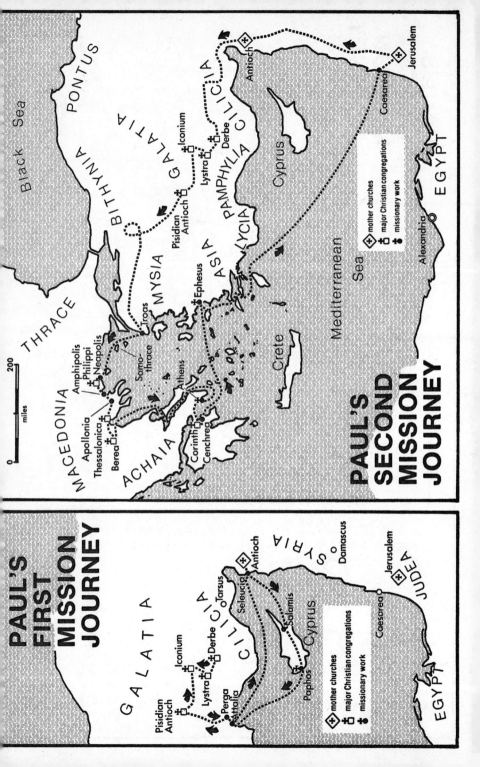

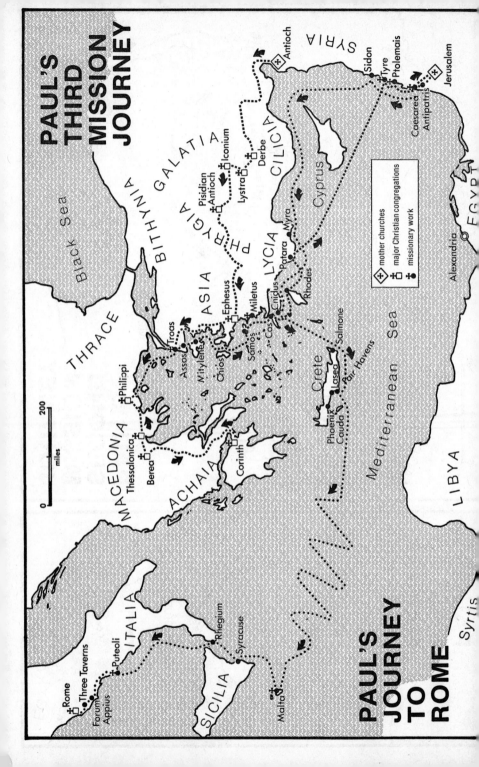